POURED OUT

"What an interesting thesis, that is, that the waning of Christendom makes possible our reclaiming of the work of the Holy Spirit by forcing the church to be in mission. Allen writes with verve and insight worthy of a theologian who attends to Scripture."

—Stanley Hauerwas, Gilbert T. Rowe Professor Emeritus of Divinity and Law, Duke University, author of *Hannah's Child*

"Two words continued to come into my mind as I read Leonard Allen's wonderful and wide-ranging *Poured Out*: "contained" and "constrained." For many, the Spirit is *contained* in the Bible, locked up by the Bible. Allen shows that approach fails the Bible itself. For the Bible's teaching is not that the Spirit is *contained* by the Bible. Rather, whatever the Spirit does will be *constrained* by the Bible, that is, consistent with the Bible. The Bible constrains us today to welcome the Spirit who has always been missional, transforming, and empowering."

—Scot McKnight, Northern Seminary, author of *The Kingdom Conspiracy*

"A well written, theologically informed, and missionally challenging book on the Holy Spirit. . . . It reflects an experiential grasp of the subject, and created desire in my heart for the things of the Spirit . . . . a book that is vital for the well-being of the church—both Pentecostal/ the Charismatic traditions and all the rest of the church."

—Berten Waggoner, former National Director, Vineyard USA

"Our approach to the Spirit can too easily become a jumble of reactions and over-corrections, adding to the ways humans over the centuries have tried to control this mysterious and powerful Reality. What better time than this to rediscover the Spirit and remember the postures of partnering with that Spirit? Drawing from Scripture, history, and personal experience, Leonard Allen provides an insightful guide on that journey."

—Mandy Smith, pastor and author of *The Vulnerable Pastor*

In *Poured Out*, Leonard Allen offers an important voice to Western Christianity's emerging conversation about the Spirit. Allen's view of how believers cooperate with the Spirit for redemptive mission is particularly powerful. It leaves the reader dissatisfied by mere intellectual reflection and wanting to move into embodied cooperation with the Spirit in mission.

—Dan Scott, senior pastor, Christ Church Nashville

Finally, a book on the Holy Spirit that combines biblical, theological, and historical scholarship with confessional storytelling and yearning for fellowship with the Trinity.

—Greg Taylor, author and pastor, Journey Church, Tulsa, OK

POURED OUT

as inauthentic." Pope Paul VI called the widespread Catholic Charismatic movement a gift to the church.

The "third wave" of the renewal movement, as Peter Wagner called it, emerged in the 1980s and is sometimes called "neo-Charismatic." It stressed the inbreaking kingdom of God, healing as a sign of the kingdom, the casting out of demons, and the gift of prophecy. The movement was open to all the gifts of the Spirit, but viewed baptism in the Spirit not as a "second blessing" but as occurring at conversion (1 Cor. 12:13). It spoke of repeated fillings with the Spirit and viewed tongues speech as one gift among others, not as "initial evidence" of Spirit baptism.

Prominent in this "third wave" movement in the West are the large networks of churches associated with Calvary Chapel, Vineyard Christian Fellowship, and Hope Chapel. Sociologist Donald Miller called them "new paradigm churches" because they broke sharply with the dominant Western tradition and looked to first-century Christianity for a radical spirituality that undermines the cynicism and fragmentation of postmodern culture. New paradigm Christians are more comfortable, said Miller, "with an epistemology that ... is rooted in personal experience, defying the sacred-profane split that has characterized much of the modern West."

Recent estimates put the number of Pentecostal, Charismatic, and neo-Charismatic believers in the world at a staggering number. The neo-Charismatic label is used as an enormous "catch-all" category of independent congregations and movements that, though differing from classic Pentecostalism, all share an emphasis on the gifts of the Spirit and "a desire to receive more of God's empowering for the Christian life." These groups include the H to Chinese Independent Churches (estimated at 50 million) and the African Independent Churches (with 50 million).

After the explosive growth of Christianity in the Global South, it is estimated that Pentecostal/Charismatic movements in their wide diversity make up 25 to 30 percent of all professed Christians in the world. Among the more than one billion Roman Catholics around the world, about 25 percent (250 million) can be considered Charismatic in orientation, with most of them in the Global South. Both the historic and the indigenous

POURED OUT

The SPIRIT of GOD EMPOWERING THE MISSION of GOD

LEONARD ALLEN

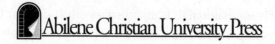
Abilene Christian University Press

POURED OUT

The Spirit of God Empowering the Mission of God

ACU
PRESS

Copyright © 2018 by Leonard Allen

ISBN 978-1-68426-130-7

Printed in the United States of America

Library of Congress Cataloguing in Publication Data is on file at the Library of Congress, Washington, DC.

Cover design by ThinkPen Design
Interior text design by Sandy Armstrong, Strong Design

For information contact:
Abilene Christian University Press
ACU Box 29138
Abilene, Texas 79699

1-877-816-4455
www.acupressbooks.com

18 19 20 21 22 23 / 7 6 5 4 3 2 1

CONTENTS

ACKNOWLEDGMENTS

This book had its beginning with an invitation from Mark Love, dean of the School of Theology and Ministry at Rochester College, to deliver two lectures on the Holy Spirit at their annual Streaming event in November 2015. I joined Among Yong, from Fuller Seminary, on the program, and his warm encouragement planted the seed of this larger project.

I also received steady encouragement along the way from Darryl Tippens, who provided critical feedback on several sections, and from Mike Cope, who proposed a rigorous timeframe in which to get this done.

My thanks also to several who read the full manuscript and provided helpful, sometimes crucial, responses: Greg Taylor, Dan Bouchelle, Kris Miller, Mandy Smith, Dan Scott, Bert Waggoner, and Rick Atchley.

Two final words of thanks: to Jason Fikes, director of ACU Press, whose deft and expert work made this better and helped meet the deadlines; and to my wife Holly whose steady support and gracious care, as always, makes my work possible.

PREFACE

[For some Christians] the Bible is the safest place for the Spirit.
That is where he belongs; not in the hurley-burley of real life.
—Michael Green

I was raised in a very conservative Christian tradition that had virtually lost the language of the Spirit. That didn't mean, of course, that we had entirely lost the Holy Spirit—for there were signs all around, as I look back, of the Spirit's presence in our community. Most obviously we were alive, our lungs filled with the breath of God. And kids like me were learning the story of God in Scripture, witnessing the lives of people who had followed Jesus seriously for many years, experiencing baptism and newness of life, gathering weekly at the "Lord's table" to share in Christ's body and blood, and being trained to "love not the world or the things of the world." But the grammar of the Spirit was missing. Almost entirely.

Songs from the Spirit

I vividly remember the young preacher at our church who baptized me when I was eleven. He was tall and thin, his face angular, with a prominent Adam's apple. There was an earnestness and appealing awkwardness about him. We had two services and two sermons on Sundays in those days, and I remember the Sunday evening when, for his sermon, he simply read the Sermon on the Mount. As an eleven-year-old boy I liked that.

I don't recall that he ever talked about the Spirit of God in his sermons, though I'm sure he read the words "Holy Spirit" or "Spirit of Christ" when

POURED OUT

they appeared in the day's sermon text. Years later, when I was in graduate school, I learned that he had struggled with alcohol, left his family, and eventually taken his own life. I was shocked and deeply saddened, yet I was only beginning to learn how such things could happen.

Regarding the Spirit, we were almost like those disciples at Ephesus who, when asked by Paul if they had received the Holy Spirit when they believed, answered, "No, we have not even heard that there is a Holy Spirit" (Acts 19:2). Okay, we had *heard* of the Holy Spirit. But we were told that the Spirit and the Scriptures—ever since the first century—were one and the same. At least that's how I heard it as a kid. And we were taught that baptism was followed by the "gift of the Holy Spirit"—though I don't remember ever being told what that might be. I surmised it was probably the Bible.

Singing was important to us, and our church was pretty good at it. I heard Colossians 3:16 a lot: "teach and admonish one another with all wisdom through psalms, hymns, and songs from the Spirit, singing to God with gratitude in your hearts." I remember a few hymns we sang that, even at the time, I realized didn't fit our doctrine—like the stanza that said, "Beyond the sacred page I seek thee Lord; my spirit pants for thee, O living Word." Or this one that we sang a lot:

> Be with me, Lord! No other gift or blessing
> Thou couldst bestow could with this one compare—
> A constant sense of Thy abiding presence,
> Where'er I am, to feel that Thou art near.

These songs not only helped correct our theology but themselves served as strong sacraments of the Spirit's presence. Maybe these were the "songs from the Spirit."

During those growing-up years, my English grammar became really good. But my theological grammar remained somewhat deficient—though I learned to speak Christian well enough to get by.

No Longer a Cinderella

Through my long engagement with the Christian history of the West, I've come to see that the theological deficiency of my own upbringing is not

12

so strange or unusual. Dallas Willard gave a name to the doctrine of the Spirit on which I was raised: Bible deism—the view that one "experiences" the Spirit solely through implanting the words, the ideas, of the Bible in one's mind. Though Bible deism is a somewhat extreme stance, churches in the West have tended to operate with a deficient doctrine of the Spirit, as we will see in the chapters ahead.

More than fifty years ago, one writer on the Spirit observed that the "doctrine of the Holy Spirit has long been a Cinderella of theology. It has suffered from much neglect and has always been one of the most difficult doctrines to discuss."[1] That has changed. The doctrine is still a challenging one; indeed, Wolfhart Pannenberg, one of the leading theologians of the later twentieth century, remarked that he thought the doctrine of the Spirit was one of the most difficult theological topics to address. He's probably right. But in recent decades the doctrine has come to the forefront of Christian thought. It is no longer a Cinderella at the Christian ball.

Why has this dramatic change occurred? In Chapter One I attempt to answer that question—and my answer may surprise you. Further, I focus on a key dimension in this renewal: recovery of "the intrinsic missionary character of the Holy Spirit."[2] That is, the pouring out of the Spirit at Pentecost, fulfilling God's promises through the prophets, was to empower, equip, and guide the church as it continues the mission of Christ throughout the world. The Spirit is God's missionary. The Spirit of God empowers and guides the mission of God. This book seeks to show how the one relates to the other.

Beginning with Astonishment

At the heart of our faith are the mystery, the wonder, and the experience of the love of God—the perfect love shared among Father, Spirit, and Son, and opened to us through the faithful mission of Christ and the continuing mission of the Spirit. This love, Scripture declares, has been "poured into our hearts through the Holy Spirit, who has been given to us" (Rom. 5:5).

God's love "poured into our hearts." We must begin with wonder, with astonishment.

That's what the apostle Paul did. Man of the Spirit and theologian of mission, he frequently bursts into praise and wonder at God's love and purposes for creation.

> Oh, the depth of the riches of the wisdom and knowledge of God!
>> How unsearchable his judgments,
>> And his paths beyond tracing out!
> "Who has known the mind of the Lord?"
> For from him and through him and to him are all things.
> (Rom. 11:33–34, 36)

Karl Barth thought that astonishment was a necessary accompaniment to the work of Christian theology. "A quite specific astonishment stands at the beginning of every theological inquiry," he said late in his life, after writing thousands of pages of theology. "If such astonishment is lacking, the whole enterprise of even the best theologian would canker at the root. On the other hand, as long as even a poor theologian is capable of astonishment, he is not lost to the fulfillment of the task. He remains serviceable as long as the possibility is left open that astonishment may seize him like an armed man."[3]

I want you to know that I am leaving that possibility wide open.

Gendered Language and the Spirit

Now to a matter of grammar. What pronoun shall we use for the Spirit? In English we have three choices: he, she, or it. The most common Hebrew word for Spirit in the Old Testament is feminine. The basic Greek word in the New Testament is neuter, and the pronoun *it* is sometimes used. But the word *Paraclete*, used by John, is masculine and is sometimes referred to as *he*. Biblical usage leaves the question open.

Using *it* seems to downplay the personhood of the Spirit. For Christians the Spirit is a someone, not a something. Using *she* is attractive because of the qualities—comforting, encouraging, nourishing—traditionally associated with the feminine, and with the Spirit. But the Father and the Son also display such qualities. Using *he* has its downside, since it easily carries the freight of human patriarchy. Thus I have chosen, for the most part, not to use a pronoun but to speak simply of "the Spirit."[4]

God is beyond gender, neither male nor female. We are challenged today, in our thinking about God, to move beyond the binary of male/female. God has been revealed to us in Scripture as Father, Spirit, and Son, and also as Creator, Comforter, and Redeemer. God is Trinity. We should not jettison the language of revelation, but at the same time seek to critique and lay down the distorting baggage of human patriarchy.[5]

Four Glimpses

I close this preface with four quick glimpses into the focus and thrust of this book.

First, the Holy Spirit is not a junior member of the Trinity. Indeed, I put forth the claim that the role or mission of the Spirit is equal in importance to the mission of Jesus the Son. The two missions are distinct but deeply intertwined. What does this mean, and how does it impact our teaching of the faith?

Second, the Holy Spirit is the power of God's inbreaking reign or kingdom. Permeating the New Testament is the claim that disciples of Jesus live in the overlap of two ages: this present age and the age to come, the "already" and the "not yet." The Spirit is the presence and power of this inbreaking age to come. The diminishment or loss of this sense of inbreaking has big consequences for the church and its mission, which we will explore in depth in the chapters to come.

Third, the Holy Spirit is no tame spirit—not the "shy member" of the Trinity. The Spirit presses the people of God relentlessly toward "new creation," shaking up the status quo, bestowing "power from on high," aiding the putting-to-death process in the untransformed places of our lives, and "groaning" with us as we join with the groaning creation.

Fourth, the Holy Spirit is the "giver of life," the Spirit of resurrection and new life. To be filled with this Spirit is to be lifted up out of apathy, defeat, and despair, and to become fruitful again. As in Ezekiel's vision of the dry bones, the Spirit comes like a wind from the four corners of the earth to bring new life.

The unprecedented interest in and focus on the Spirit of God in our time, combined with the unprecedented explosion of Christian faith throughout the Global South, should tell us something. Perhaps for us in the West it is at least this: "Only by attending to the Spirit are we going to be able to move beyond sterile, rationalistic, powerless religion and recover the intimacy with God our generation longs for."[6]

NOTES

[1] Arthur Wainwright, *The Trinity in the New Testament* (London: SPCK, 1962), 199.

[2] David Bosch, *Transforming Mission: Paradigm Shifts in the Theology of Mission*, 20th anniversary edition (1991; Maryknoll, NY: Orbis, 2011), 116.

[3] Karl Barth, *Evangelical Theology: An Introduction* (1963; Grand Rapids: Eerdmans, 1979), 64.

[4] Gordon Fee, in his magisterial work, *God's Empowering Presence: The Holy Spirit in the Letters of Paul* (Peabody, MA: Hendrickson, 1994), chose to use *he*; Alasdair Heron, in *The Holy Spirit* (Philadelphia: Westminster, 1983), uses *it*; and Eugene Rogers, in *After the Spirit* (Grand Rapids: Eerdmans, 2005), uses *she*.

[5] For in-depth treatment of this issue, see Alvin F. Kimmel, ed., *This Is My Name Forever: The Trinity and Gender Language for God* (Downers Grove, IL: InterVarsity, 2001), especially the essay by Stanley Grenz, "Is God Sexual?" For a briefer treatment, see Robin Parry, "Two Men and an It: Is the Triune God Male?," in *Worshipping Trinity*, 2nd edition (Eugene, OR: Cascade, 2012), 188–97.

[6] Clark Pinnock, *Flame of Love: A Theology of the Holy Spirit* (Downers Grove, IL: InterVarsity, 1996), 19.

(UN)CONTAINED

The doctrine of the Spirit, long neglected in the West, has come to the forefront as Christendom has collapsed and God's mission is renewed.

In the Global South, they struggle to keep up with the Spirit; in the West, we struggle to embrace it.
—Diana Butler Bass

It is the nature of the Holy Spirit to shake up the church, particularly when the church becomes self-satisfied and content with the status quo.
—Stanley Hauerwas and William Willimon

The Holy Spirit is no tame Spirit. When the people of God grow comfortable, satisfied, maybe sleepy and bored; when they think they have things pretty much nailed down in their creeds and noncreeds; when the call of God's mission to the whole world, especially to the broken and the poor, recedes, it is the tendency of the Spirit to shake up the church and dislodge it from its ease and self-satisfaction.

This shake-up is happening to many churches in the West in this season. Many will die. And through the shaking, many will renew or discover a sense of the expansive mission of God and new openness to the Spirit of God.

Scripture tells us that the Spirit of God was active in creation, hovering over and bringing order out of chaos. After the work of creation, Scripture speaks of the "pouring out" of the Spirit, ranging from Old Testament promise to New Testament fulfillment. It's a vivid metaphor connoting the lavish and life-giving gift of God's love and renewing energy. The focus of the outpouring is renewal of God's mission, originally given to the people of Israel, to be "a light to the nations." Following Pentecost, the Spirit, at every turn, guided and empowered the continuation of that mission to the nations and for the renewal of creation. What happened to the Spirit of Pentecost in the church?

Wondering Where the Spirit Went

In the post-biblical period, we can see two main streams regarding the role of the Spirit in the church, flowing alongside and mingling with each other—one we could call dynamic/charismatic and the other more "institutional" and ordered. In the first 150 years or so, the first stream seems to have constituted the "mainstream" of the Christian movement, while the second stream eventually became strongly predominant.[1]

The more institutional type became overwhelmingly dominant with the emergence of Christendom. Christendom was born when, in the early fourth century, Roman emperor Constantine was "converted" and declared Christian faith the preferred religion of the empire. Very quickly the status of the church changed from a frequently persecuted minority to an emperor-approved majority. By the end of the fourth century, it was illegal *not* to be a Christian. The church quickly came to occupy a dominant place in Western culture. For almost 1,500 years there would be a state church, upheld by law—an arrangement often called *Constantinianism* or, more popularly, *Christendom*.

This new church-state relationship brought profound transformation to the church. The church's status evolved from a persecuted minority to an imperial power that persecuted the dissidents in its midst. Its character gradually changed from a Spirit-empowered contrast-society to an institutionalized society reflecting the bureaucracy of the Roman government. Through this process, there were changes in the understanding of the church, the nature of the church's mission in the world, the call to discipleship, the practice of conversion, and other key practices and doctrines—including the doctrine of the Holy Spirit.

Radical Protestants have viewed this shift as the key episode precipitating the corruption and fall of the true church; mainstream Christians have tended to view it as opening the door to the strong institutions and rich cultural achievements necessary to establish the Christian faith throughout the world. A case can be made for each view. But it would be hard to deny that in either interpretation the result was deep compromises of the faith, unholy alliances, and countless betrayals of the gospel.

In the Constantinian shift, two prominent features of the Spirit in the New Testament were diminished. First is the Spirit's central role in the inbreaking of the *eschaton*, God's long-promised new age. In the New Testament, the focus of the Spirit is not simply on relating a person individually to God and applying Christ's death to the believer, but on beginning to realize within the present age the life of the coming age. The Spirit is the power of the inbreaking reign of God. Second, and closely related, is the Spirit's role in creating community among the people of God: what the New Testament calls "the fellowship of the Holy Spirit" (2 Cor. 13:14). In Christendom, the church came to be conceived essentially as an institution mediating grace to the individual rather than as the Spirit-filled community enjoying the mutuality and giftedness of the "fellowship of the Spirit." The focus of the Spirit was to guarantee apostolicity, Scripture's authority, and the effectiveness of the sacraments as channels of grace.

The churches that came out of the Protestant Reformation tended to maintain a similar view of the Spirit. The reformers focused on three primary works of the Spirit: in the interpretation and preaching of the Word, in the practice of the sacraments, and in the application of Christ's atoning death to the believer. The Spirit inspired the apostles and prophets, and through the preaching of inspired Scripture illuminates the minds of those who hear the Word. Through Word and sacrament, the Spirit applied Christ's work of redemption to believers, thereby seeking to form them in the way of Christ. Though the Spirit received renewed and needed emphasis in these three ways, the Protestant churches continued the Constantinian trend of diminishing the two prominent features of the Spirit in the New Testament: there was less emphasis on both the inbreaking of the new age and the Spirit's role in fellowship.

The mainstream Western tradition, when measured against the New Testament, was marked by a notable deficiency in its doctrine of the Spirit. The New Testament emphasizes the present eschatological work of the Spirit, and the Spirit's freedom and dynamism in the community; later Christian tradition tended to institutionalize the Spirit and assume that Christians were mostly only *preparing* for the end, not already *partaking* partially of it. So the church becomes more of a holding tank—a place to wait for rescue and for heaven.

In the Christendom centuries, says Alan Kreider, "Christians could coast along on autopilot. . . . Without a sense of providence and eschatology, many Christians became functional deists; their God was a cosmic clockmaker who was uninvolved in human events and would not intervene in history disruptively, creatively, hopefully, to bring about impossible reconciliation. As a result, many Christians were docile, tractable participants in the status quo of a society that was, after all, Christian."[2] Or as Richard Rohr put it (with some hyperbole), "The vast majority of Christian ministry [in the West] has been concerned with 'churching' people into symbolic, restful, and usually ethnic belonging systems rather than any real spiritual transformation into the mystery of God."[3]

To be sure, beginning in the fourth century, new monastic movements kept mission alive, mostly around the margins of Christendom. They sought to evangelize and educate the pagan tribes of Europe and assimilate them into the expanding Christian culture. But by and large, the churches of the Christendom centuries were no longer pilgrim churches, venturing out in the world as witnesses to the inbreaking of God's reign and embodying the new way of life made possible by the resurrection of the Messiah and the pouring out of the Spirit. And because they were no longer pilgrim or missionary churches, the doctrine of the Spirit was contained, now redefined by the settled caretaker role that the empire required.

In contrast, in the New Testament we see the Spirit as the dynamic force and guide for the mission of God, beginning in Jerusalem, extending to Judea and Samaria, and to the ends of the earth (Acts 1:8). The diminishment of this dynamic sense of mission corresponds with a narrowed and tamed doctrine of the Spirit. The two diminishments go hand in hand.

Mission, as a result, became secondary or even peripheral to the vision of the church in the West. The early nineteenth century saw the emergence of a new missionary movement in the West that gained considerable momentum by the end of the century; but it took place largely outside the institutional churches of late Christendom—and often in opposition to them. At the same time, this movement tended to carry with it a Western institutional vision of the church.

The doctrine of the Spirit remained anemic. And mission remained, at best, a sideline in the life of traditional churches. Both the Spirit and the mission were contained.

What Changed?

By the later twentieth century, something had changed. As a result, the doctrine of the Spirit remains no longer the awkward stepchild of theology but has risen as the center of attention. As one prominent writer on the Spirit notes, "Never before in the history of Christian doctrine has there been so wide and varied interest in, and at times almost an enthusiasm for, the Holy Spirit." And not only among theologians. As another writer says, "Many Christians desire to encounter a Holy Spirit who brings new life to their spirits in the concrete circumstances of their lives and who renews the face of the earth as we enter the third millennium."[4]

What changed? Why the unprecedented interest in and focus on the Holy Spirit at this time?

Of course, for well over a century, the Pentecostal and later the Charismatic renewal movements have been on the front edge of interest in the Spirit, and beginning in the 1950s and 1960s, these movements widely impacted the mainline Protestant and Roman Catholic churches. In the 1980s and 90s a "third wave" of the Spirit widely impacted Evangelical churches. Furthermore, in the second half of the twentieth century, as we are learning, there was a revolutionary shift in Christianity's center of gravity. It was a shift away from the West and North to the Global South, where Christianity has been expanding at breakneck speed, mostly in Pentecostal/Charismatic form. And it will almost certainly continue to do so.[5]

But the interest in and openness to the Spirit has been breaking out of these historic streams. The distinction between Charismatic and non-Charismatic streams is blurring somewhat. Pentecostals and Charismatics are becoming more self-critical, and the historic non-Charismatic and anti-Charismatic streams are realizing that the Spirit's presence and power are not secondary but central to the Christian life and the mission of God.

Thus we have more and more theologians saying things like this:

The church lives not by savvy, worldly wisdom, and techniques for church growth but rather lives moment by moment, in every time and place, utterly dependent on the gifts of the Holy Spirit. Thus the Holy Spirit is nothing less than a life-and-death matter for the people of God. . . .

"Come, Holy Spirit!" is the first and last prayer of the church, our only hope in life and death. In receiving the gift of the Spirit, we can begin the adventure of discipleship and end all our attempts at self-justification.[6]

I see at least five reasons for the dramatic shift. *First, and most significant, is that Christendom has collapsed, and in North America "neo-Christendom" has sharply receded.*[7] I believe this broad focus on the Spirit is happening now because of the growing sense that we are on mission in a new landscape—after Christendom and, in America, after an unofficial, functional Christendom. And there is a growing sense that we in the West have recoveries to make.

It is just beginning to hit us that in North America we are living in a post-(neo-)Christendom culture. The cultural status and power that Christianity in America held from about the 1850s to the 1960s has sharply receded. Christians of all stripes are now being forced to disengage from the old establishment habits that have enabled them to feel so comfortable and at home in American culture. And as these old habits are being broken, Christians' true identity as strangers and pilgrims is being renewed, and ways of being the church more suited to the status of "strangers and exiles" are fitfully emerging.

Stuart Murray's definition has become standard: "Post-Christendom is the culture that emerges as the Christian faith loses coherence within a society that has been definitively shaped by the Christian story and as the institutions that have been developed to express Christian convictions decline in influence."[8] In Christendom, the church occupied a central and influential place in society; after Christendom, it gets pushed to the margins, out of its accustomed place of power and control. And that's where we find ourselves now—more and more on the margins of cultural power.

So let's be clear. Any sort of Christian establishment has conclusively ended. As David Bentley Hart recently put it, "we now live in the time after Christendom, among the rapidly vanishing fragments of its material culture, bound to it by only a few lingering habits of thought."[9]

Christianity's loss of cultural power in America is waking Christians up to the reality that we are in a missionary situation in our own culture—or in any culture. And this is forcing us to rethink our mission, our theology, and our priorities.

We now find ourselves in a situation in certain ways like that of the pre-Constantinian church of the first three centuries. Christians are being forced into a situation where they again must lean by faith on God's governance of history rather than America's governance of it, and must confess with new seriousness that Jesus, not Caesar, that Jesus, not modern democracy, is Lord.

When we've been living more or less comfortably in a culture that has sanctioned our faith, even propped it up for us, what do we need the Holy Spirit for—except the occasional sweetness of the Spirit's private comfort? But when we find ourselves more and more on the margins, faced with the status of strangers and exiles, out of power and out of favor, it begins to dawn on us that we truly need the power of God's Spirit to live on God's mission.

Second, the stage for this shift was set by the renewal of the doctrine of the Trinity in the twentieth century. The doctrine of the Trinity had been in steady recession in the modern period. With the rise and eventual dominance of the scientific worldview, where "reasonableness" became the new standard of truth, the Trinity was viewed more and more as an irrelevant mystery. Some Christian leaders became hostile to the doctrine and many became indifferent. The recovery of this central Christian doctrine was launched in the early twentieth century by Karl Barth, and he was followed by many other theologians from a variety of traditions, who have advanced this recovery in rich and powerful ways.

What has emerged from these efforts is a recovery of God's relationality—between Father, Son, and Spirit in the life of the Trinity, and in the outpouring of God's love upon human beings. In this view, God is understood as a community of persons. God is not a solitary being who rules through arbitrary exercise of power, but rather the perfect model of loving community—becoming vulnerable, sharing the divine life, loving like a perfect parent. Part of this recovery, of course, has been a fuller sense of the Spirit's distinct role in the life of the Trinity and in making it possible for human beings to share that life.

Third, the context in the West for this shift was the decline of the modern worldview and the emergence of what is often called a "postmodern" outlook. For more than two centuries, Christian faith has been on the defensive against the steady encroachment of the secular and scientific worldview. Christian intellectuals and apologists have, to varying degrees, sought to accommodate that worldview. But now, with the decline of the modern worldview, a new landscape has allowed more openness to the transcendent and spiritual realm. The prestige of scientific definitions of reality has been diminishing; the invisible spiritual realm has been making a comeback for Western people.

One example: from the 1960s to the 1990s, interest in and openness to the miraculous dramatically increased in North America. In 1995, for example, a *Time* magazine poll found that 69 percent of all Americans believed in the possibility of miracles in the world today. This development, Robert Mullin argued, was one of the most remarkable occurrences in American Christianity in the second half of the twentieth century.[10]

But as Charles Taylor has argued, this openness is not so much to traditional Christian belief. Rather, what marks the spiritual landscape in the West is the proliferation of middle ways between the two poles of affirming traditional belief and rejecting it. We are surrounded by what

Taylor calls "cross-pressures"—the swirling presence of multiple and contested options for ultimate meaning and human flourishing. "We are torn,"
he says, "between an anti-Christian thrust and a repulsion towards some
extreme form of reduction; so we invent new positions." The result is a
more fluid and fragile faith, a "diffusive Christianity," a believing without
belonging. A new age of spiritual searching has emerged—one in which
people are not constrained by traditional forms, doctrines, and boundaries. "Our age is very far from settling into a comfortable unbelief. Although
many individuals do so, and more still seem to be on the outside, the
unrest continues to surface. Could it ever be otherwise? The secular age
is schizophrenic, or better, deeply cross-pressured. People seem at a safe
distance from religion; and yet they are very moved to know that there are
dedicated believers."[11]

Fourth, the explosion of Christian faith in the Global South has been a
key factor in the shift. The recovery of a larger place for the Spirit in God's
mission has been greatly stimulated by the non-Western churches. In the
past several generations, it has become clear that Pentecostal, Charismatic,
and indigenous Christian movements have taken center stage in the worldwide movement of Christianity. These movements are windswept with
the vibrancy and unpredictability of the Spirit. They are both messy and
powerfully effective, both offensive to many Western Christians and missionally dynamic. Phillip Jenkins notes that amid the great diversity of
churches in the Global South, one of the most visible common features
is "the critical idea that God intervenes directly in everyday life."[12] These
churches have not been "disenchanted" by Western secularization, and so
expect God to work within the basic assumptions of their own cultures—
cultures that are populated with spirits and in which the Holy Spirit enters
as Lord.

These churches and movements have been powerfully evangelistic,
especially among the poor and marginalized peoples of the world. They
have also shown an impressive breadth of social concern. Overturning
the common impression that Pentecostals tend to be otherworldly and
neglectful of justice and social well-being, Donald Miller has documented
the breadth of social concern in global Pentecostalism—medical services,

education, counseling, economic development, compassion ministries, and work for justice.[13]

Fifth, a final reason for the shift was the renewal of mission as a centerpiece of Christian faith. Over the centuries of Christendom, as noted previously, the established churches were not missionary churches. They were mostly caretakers of a "Christian" culture. Renewal movements arose from time to time, the largest of which was John Wesley's Methodist movement beginning in the 1730s, and they generated strong missional energy. Around 1800, a growing missionary movement emerged, but it had an ambivalent relationship to the churches of late Christendom. It emerged mostly outside those churches and outside the clergy, using voluntary societies or what we would call parachurch organizations and "laymen" as leaders. As the movement gained headway and momentum in the nineteenth century, churches began to be awakened and become involved, but missions became mostly a "department" or program of the church, not the center of its vision and life.

In the early to mid-twentieth century, a profound reorientation took place in the understanding of Christian mission. Mission came to be viewed not as one (perhaps important) aspect of the church's life, but as the very centerpiece of what God is up to in the world. Mission was an attribute of the Triune God. The Father through the Spirit sent the Son into the world out of the depths of divine love, the Spirit was poured out to continue that mission, and the Son sends his followers into the world in the power of the Spirit. Jesus prayed to his Father, "As you sent me into the world, I have sent them into the world" (John 17:18), and later declared to his disciples, "'Peace be with you! As the Father sent me, I am sending you.' And with that he breathed on them and said, 'Receive the Holy Spirit'" (20:21–22). Mission came to be understood as the Trinity-in-mission. The term *missio Dei* became the shorthand for this missional revolution.[14]

The Missional Spirit

The diminishment of mission and of the Spirit's work in the Christendom centuries went hand in hand; so it is that after (neo-)Christendom the recovery of mission and of the Spirit go hand in hand. With the breakdown of

Christendom in Europe and the receding of a functional Christendom in North America in the twentieth century, and with the emergence of an unprecedented new global Christianity, a strong new sense of focus on and engagement in the mission of God is emerging. And it should not surprise us that with this emergence, focus on the Holy Spirit—God's missionary—has come to the forefront in recent decades. The Spirit of God empowers and guides the mission of God. In this book I want to show how the one relates to the other.

The mission of the Triune God is the starting point for the church's call to mission. The Father sent Jesus, Israel's Messiah, into the world in the power of the Holy Spirit for the salvation of the world. Or we can say that the Spirit of the Father, poured out by the Son (following his resurrection and ascension), works to bring a broken creation back through the Son to the Father. Following Pentecost, the mission of the Spirit is to empower and complete the reconciliation of all creation to the Father through the ministry of Jesus the Son.

So mission is not essentially a (sometimes neglected) program of the church or an initiative that the church decides to undertake (or not); rather, the church, as it welcomes the Spirit, participates in and lives out the mission initiated by the Triune God.

So thorough was the separation of the Spirit from mission—and so diminished were both—over the Christendom centuries, that "a gradual rediscovery of the intrinsic missionary character of the Holy Spirit" has occurred only in the twentieth century.[15]

In the mission of God, Scripture bears witness to two sendings: the sending of the Son and the sending of the Spirit. The mission of Christ is set alongside the mission of the Spirit (see Gal. 4:4–6). God sent his Son to redeem and make possible adoption to sonship, and God sent the Spirit of his Son to us, who enables us to call out "*Abba*, Father." Further, Paul stated, "No one can say 'Jesus is Lord' except by the Holy Spirit" (1 Cor. 12:3). The mission of the Spirit, among other things, is to initiate people into relationship with the Trinity: the Father as *Abba* and Jesus as Lord. The mission of Christ and the mission of the Spirit are "intertwined and equal; one is not major and the other minor. . . . The two are partners in the work of redemption."[16] Their missions are distinct, but Christ and the Spirit are each deeply engaged and present in the mission of the other.

So we are learning to speak of the Spirit of mission or the missional Spirit. We are learning to identify the Spirit as the power and guide of God's mission. In the West, which has been deeply resistant to the Spirit of God in modernity, Christians are slowly beginning to welcome the Spirit in the call to mission.

Poured Out

Needed now, I think, is further recovery of Scripture's bold and lavish language of "pouring out." The image of outpouring is a prominent one to portray the mission of the Spirit in the age of the Messiah (italics added):

> For I will pour water on the thirsty land,
> and streams on the dry ground;
> I will *pour out* my Spirit on your offspring,
> and my blessing on your descendants.
> (Isa. 44:3)

> When I have brought them back from the nations and have gathered them from the countries of their enemies, I will be proved holy through them in the sight of many nations. Then they will know that I am the LORD their God, ... I will no longer hide my face from them, for I will *pour out* my Spirit on the people of Israel, declares the Sovereign LORD. (Ezek. 39:27–29)

> And afterward,
> I will *pour out* my Spirit on all people.
> Your sons and daughters will prophesy,
> your old men will dream dreams,
> your young men will see visions.
> Even on my servants, both men and women,
> I will *pour out* my Spirit in those days. (Joel 2:28–29)

God has raised this Jesus to life, and we are all witnesses of it. Exalted to the right hand of God, he has received from the Father the promised Holy Spirit and has *poured out* what you now see and hear. (Acts 2:32–33)

While Peter was still speaking these words, the Holy Spirit came on all who heard the message. The circumcised believers who had come with Peter were astonished that the gift of the Holy Spirit had been *poured out* even on Gentiles. (Acts 10:44–45)

He saved us through the washing of rebirth and renewal by the Holy Spirit, whom he *poured out* on us generously through Jesus our Savior (Titus 3:5–6)

We boast in the hope of the glory of God. Not only so, but we also glory in our sufferings, because we know that suffering produces perseverance; perseverance, character; and character, hope. And hope does not put us to shame, because God's love has been *poured out* into our hearts through the Holy Spirit, who has been given to us. (Rom. 5:2–5)

Poured out. It's an image of lavish generosity, of breadth and richness and fullness. It's not a sparing gift here and there, reserved for a few lone prophets, extraordinary leaders, and wild visionaries. On the day of Pentecost, Peter, claiming fulfillment of Joel's prophecy, announced that the outpouring of the Spirit was not restricted to a few special people but was being poured out on the whole community of God's people and beyond—sons, daughters, old men, young men, servants, male and female.

But Peter clearly didn't know the full implications of the prophecy he cited. Certainly the apostles received this outpouring: "what seemed to be tongues of fire . . . separated and came to rest on each of them. All of them were filled with the Holy Spirit" (Acts 2:3-4). Later, in response to Peter's announcement about the Messiah, three thousand Jews were baptized and received the gift of the Spirit (2:38). Luke completes his reference to Joel 2 in verse 39, adding an allusion to Isaiah 57:19, saying that the same promise is "for all who are far off"—a clear reference to the inclusion of the Gentiles.

But Peter didn't yet understand. After being called to the gentile Cornelius's house by a vision, Peter preached and saw the Spirit poured out again. Peter and all the circumcised believers with him were astonished that "the gift of the Holy Spirit had been poured out even on Gentiles" (Acts 10:45). It was dawning on Peter that, as Joel and Isaiah had said, the pouring out of the Spirit was for everyone, including "all who are far off." It was a momentous turning point. Believers all over Judea began to hear the news: *The gentiles received the Spirit, just as we did in the beginning!* "So if God gave them the same gift he gave us, who believed in the Lord Jesus Christ," Peter concluded, "who was I to think that I could stand in God's way?" (Acts 11:15, 17).

The Spirit of Jesus unleashed the energy of God's mission in the world and will not be limited only to a select few. The mission is broad—as wide as the created order—and God's Spirit is poured out on all believers to give them new life and enable them to participate in that creation-wide mission.

The Holy Spirit, of course, is not a liquid but a person. *Pouring out* is a metaphor for the lavish and life-giving gift of the Spirit to all believers in the messianic age that has dawned. A corollary metaphor, sometimes combined with it, is "living water." In the Old Testament, God is called "the fountain of living waters" (Jer. 2:13) and the "fountain of life" (Ps. 36:9). "I will pour water upon the thirsty land," says Yahweh through Isaiah, "and streams upon the dry ground; I will *pour* my Spirit upon your descendants, and my blessing on your offspring" (Isa. 44:3—italics mine). The landscape will be a wasteland "till the Spirit is poured on us from on high, and the desert becomes a fertile field, and the fertile field seems like a forest" (Isa. 32:15). And there is Jesus' invitation: "Let anyone who is thirsty come to me and drink. Whoever believes in me, as the Scripture has said, rivers of living water will flow from within them." "By this he meant the Spirit, whom those who believed in him were later to receive" (John 7:37–38).

If the Spirit has been often constricted and contained—quenched—in the Christian tradition in the West, these images of lavish outpouring can open new possibilities of reclamation and fullness and life. And they can help us make further and fuller connections between the Spirit of God and the mission of God.

Many years ago, Emil Brunner said, "The church exists by mission, just as a fire exists by burning. Where there is no mission, there is no Church; and where there is neither Church nor mission, there is no faith."[17] As a church's sense of participation in God's mission declines, the Spirit is quenched and the church weakens. It becomes club-like, inward focused, comfortable, squeamish about outsiders, and . . . bored and sleepy.

The impulse is strong to contain and control the Spirit—by our own tastes and sensibilities, by the comfortable inertia of our traditions, and by the deep assumptions of our culture in the West. But "a church that seeks to restrict and control the Spirit, as too dangerous and unpredictable, may be safe, but it has signed its own death warrant."[18]

A choice lies before us. We can continue to contain the Spirit, which is tantamount to spiritual death, or we can, like millions around the globe, open our lives to the Spirit's outpouring, bringing new possibilities of reclamation and fullness and life.

NOTES

[1] James D. G. Dunn, *Unity and Diversity in the New Testament: An Inquiry into the Character of Earliest Christianity* (Philadelphia: Trinity Press, 1991), chapter 9.

[2] Alan and Eleanor Kreider, *Worship and Mission after Christendom* (Scottdale, PA: Herald, 2011), 118–19.

[3] Richard Rohr and Andreas Ebert, *The Enneagram: A Christian Perspective* (New York: Crossroad, 1990), xv.

[4] Veli-Matti Karkkainen, *The Holy Spirit* (Philadelphia: Fortress), 1; Elizabeth Dryer, in *Advents of the Spirit: An Introduction to the Current Study of Pneumatology*, ed. Bradford Hinze and Lyle Dabney (Milwaukee, WI: Marquette University Press, 2001), 123. Whatever a new pouring out of the Spirit might be in the West, it is at least clear that a torrent of books and articles about the Spirit is being poured out.

[5] See Philip Jenkins, *The Next Christendom: The Coming of Global Christianity* (New York: Oxford University Press, 2003), and *God's Continent: Christianity, Islam, and Europe's Religious Crisis* (New York: Oxford, 2009).

[6] Stanley Hauerwas and William Willimon, *The Holy Spirit* (Nashville: Abingdon, 2015), ix, x.

[7] "Neo-Christendom" is John Yoder's term. It fits the American situation where, though church and state were legally separated, the deep assumption of a (Protestant) Christian cultural establishment remained. *The Priestly Kingdom: Social Ethics as Gospel* (South Bend, IN: University of Notre Dame, 1984), 142.

[8] Stuart Murray, *Post-Christendom: Church and Mission in a Strange New World* (Carlisle, PA: Paternoster, 2004), 19.

[9] David Bentley Hart, "No Enduring City," *First Things* (August 2013), accessed on November 1, 2017, https://www.firstthings.com/article/2013/08/no-enduring-city/.

[10] Robert Bruce Mullin, *Miracles and the Modern Religious Imagination* (New Haven, CT: Yale University, 1996), 1–30, 262.

[11] Charles Taylor, *A Secular Age* (Cambridge, MA: Harvard, 2007), 595, 599, 518–19, 727.

[12] Jenkins, *The Next Christendom*, 77.

[13] Donald E. Miller and Tetsunao Yamamori, *Global Pentecostalism: The New Face of Christian Social Engagement* (Los Angeles: University of California, 2007).

[14] For documentation of this shift, see Norman E. Thomas, ed., *Classic Texts in Mission and World Christianity* (Maryknoll, NY: Orbis, 1995).

[15] David Bosch, *Transforming Mission: Paradigm Shifts in the Theology of Mission*, 20th anniversary edition (1991; Maryknoll, NY: Orbis, 2011), 116.

[16] Clark Pinnock, *Flame of Love: A Theology of the Holy Spirit* (Downers Grove, IL: InterVarsity, 1996), 82.

[17] Emil Brunner, *The Word in the World* (New York: Charles Scribner's Sons, 1931), 108.

[18] James Dunn, "Towards the Spirit of Christ," in *The Work of the Spirit*, ed. Michael Welker (Grand Rapids: Eerdmans, 2006), 26.

2

TRADITIONS

The doctrine of the Spirit has been diminished, in both subtle and blatant ways, in the Western Christian tradition.

To be possessed by the Holy Spirit is surely a frightening prospect. The temptation to domesticate the Spirit is almost irresistible.
—Stanley Hauerwas

The outside observer would be pardoned for thinking that the Christian doctrine of the Trinity is God the Father, Jesus the Son, and the Holy Church; or, if he looked in a different direction, . . . God the Father, Jesus the Son, and the Holy Scriptures.
—James D. G. Dunn

All of us, whether we quite know it or not, are shaped by doctrinal traditions. We may like to think that we just read and interpret the Bible for ourselves. But one's approach to the Bible and to Christian doctrine always touches some trajectory—some tradition—of interpretation. It's better to know something about that trajectory and began to assess it than to remain blind to it.

This holds for one's view of the Holy Spirit. So in this chapter, I briefly survey five major streams in order to provide a sense of how the Spirit has been understood in Christian history.

Christendom Traditions

As we saw in Chapter One, two main streams regarding the role of the Spirit in the church emerged. One was more dynamic/charismatic, the other more "institutional" and ordered. The streams, we can say, gradually began to diverge. With the emergence of Christendom, the institutional type that had been developing for some time quickly triumphed. As we saw, the church evolved from a Spirit-empowered contrast-society to an institution reflecting the bureaucracy of the Roman government.

The doctrine of the Spirit began to develop in this context. It lagged well behind the doctrines of the Trinity and of Christ, primarily due to the fact that it was not the subject of prolonged and intense controversy, as were the issues of Christ's relationship to the Father and the relationship of the divine and human in Christ. The Nicene Creed (AD 325) contained only the one line ". . . and in the Holy Spirit." But in the mid-fourth century, controversy over the deity of the Spirit broke out, and in response, Basil the Great, bishop of Caesarea, wrote the first full-length book on the Spirit (about AD 375). He argued that the Spirit should receive the same status and glory as the Father and the Son, "for the Holy Spirit partakes of the fullness of deity." As a result, the Council of Constantinople in AD 381 added an expanded clause to the Nicene Creed: it affirmed "the Holy Spirit, the Lord and giver of life, who proceeds from the Father, who with the Father and the Son together is worshiped and glorified, who spoke by the prophets."

From this point in the late fourth century, the doctrine of the Spirit took shape in two different trajectories in Christendom—one in the Western Church (centered in Rome) and the other in the Eastern Church (centered in Constantinople).

For the Western Church, Augustine of Hippo (AD 354–430) was the predominant influence. His magisterial *On the Trinity* has been the most influential work on the Trinity in the West. His understanding of the Spirit is set in this Trinitarian frame. He had two favorite designations for the Spirit. One was the Spirit as the bond of love between the Father and the Son. He recognized on the basis of passages like 1 John 4:7–19 and Romans 5:5 that each member of the Trinity can be called *Love*, but thought that the name was particularly appropriate for the Spirit as the bond of love uniting Father and Son. "The Holy Spirit . . . is neither of the Father alone, nor of the Son alone, but of both . . . a mutual love, wherewith the Father and the Son reciprocally love one another."[1]

His other prominent name for the Spirit was *Gift*, drawing on New Testament passages like Acts 2:38, which specifically speaks of the Spirit as "gift." As Gift, the Spirit is the source of grace in the believer's life, enabling him or her to reverse the curse of the fall—which is disordered love—and to grow in love for and delight in God. For Augustine, the three names of the third person of the Trinity were Holy Spirit, Love, and Gift.

Another key focus in Augustine's doctrine of the Spirit was his insistence on what was called the "double procession" of the Spirit. The revision to the Nicene Creed in 381 included the phrase "who proceeds from the Father." Just as Christ was confessed to be "only begotten" of the Father, so the Spirit was said to "proceed . . . from the Father." But Augustine insisted that the Spirit proceeded "from the Father *and* the Son," a view that soon became dominant in the West. This was called the *filioque* clause ("and from the Son"), and became the source of deep tension between the Eastern and Western churches, as we will see.

Augustine placed increasing stress on the church as institution. He can speak, like the New Testament, of the church as a community of believers, but its significance recedes because he is dealing with the church's change of status with the emergence of Christendom. The church has become such a mixture of the converted and unconverted that it was no longer clear that there was a Spirit-filled, transformed community. The tendency was to see the clergy—and the growing hierarchy—as the real church, and thus to place more and more focus on the institution of the church as the mediator of grace and the Holy Spirit. So Augustine could insist that "the Holy Spirit is given by the imposition of hands in the Catholic Church only. . . ."[2]

As discussed in Chapter One in reference to the Constantinian shift, Augustine's doctrine of the Spirit further downplays the Spirit's inbreaking of the *eschaton* (the new age) and the "fellowship of the Spirit" (2 Cor. 13:14).

It can be argued that Augustine's eschatology is basically dualistic, resisting a realization of the world to come in the materiality of the present.

As Colin Gunton explains, "In Augustine we are near the beginning of the era in which the church is conceived essentially as an institution mediating grace to the individual rather than as the community formed on the analogy of the Trinity's interpersonal relationships." Augustine's theology, it is widely noted, "lacks the means to give personal distinctiveness" to the Spirit in the Trinity.[3] He viewed the Spirit as the love between the Father and the Son, and it is difficult to view the act of love between two persons as itself a person. In short, Augustine—the father of Western theology—does not give due weight to the distinctive person and role of the Spirit in the Trinity.

The churches that came out of the Protestant Reformation of the sixteenth century, as we saw in Chapter One, were rooted in the same Christendom tradition and tended to maintain a similar view. The reformers placed renewed emphasis on the Spirit's role in the preaching of the Word and in applying Christ's atoning death to the believer in response to faith. But the Protestant churches reflected the same diminishment of *eschaton* and fellowship. This diminishment was heightened in scholastic Protestantism, where the Spirit was "hardly to be experienced apart from the Bible."[4]

Kilian McDonnell characterizes the Protestant and Catholic emphasis this way: "In Protestantism, the interest in pneumatology has been largely in pietism where it is a function of interiority and inwardness. In Roman Catholicism, its dominant expression has been in books on [personal] spirituality . . . or when speaking of the structural elements of the church." He concludes that "in the West, we think essentially in Christological categories, with the Holy Spirit as an extra. . . . We decorate . . . with pneumatological baubles, a little Spirit tinsel."[5]

As noted above, the *filioque* clause—that the Spirit proceeded from both the Father *and* the *Son*—became a deep wedge between the Western Church and the Eastern Church. In the sixth century, the pope allowed the *filioque* clause to be added to the Nicene Creed without consulting the Eastern churches. They objected both to the usurpation of ecclesial authority by the pope and to the view of the Spirit that it represented. The tensions continued to mount until, in AD 1054, an official split occurred between the Roman Church in the West and the Orthodox Church in the East. The separation remains to the present day.

Orthodox bishop Kallistos (Timothy) Ware expressed the Eastern Church's predominant view of the Western tradition: "Many Orthodox feel that, as a result of the *filioque*, the Spirit in Western thought has become subordinated to the Son—if not in theory, then in practice. The West pays insufficient attention to the work of the Spirit in the world, in the church, in the daily life of each man."[6]

The Eastern Church tended to maintain a more vibrant and dynamic view of the Spirit. The three great Cappadocian fathers in the fourth century—Basil the Great, Gregory the Great, and Gregory of Nazianzus—became the three great theologians of the Spirit whose work deeply shaped the Eastern tradition.

In the Eastern Church, similar to the West, the Spirit relates closely to the institutional authority and structures of the church. But the Eastern Church holds the deep conviction that "holy tradition" in its entirety is the Spirit's work and legacy. A contemporary Eastern theologian put it concisely: "Church, tradition, and Scripture are woven into a whole, and the work of the Spirit is the soul of this integral unity." Another said, "Tradition is the witness of the Spirit, . . . the constant abiding of the Spirit and not only the memory of words. Tradition is a *charismatic*, not a historical, principle."[7] Authority is not vested mainly in a hierarchy (as with the Pope in the West) or the Scriptures (as with Protestants) or the local community (as with many independent churches); they believe that authority is focused by Jesus' sacramental presence throughout the whole body and life of the church—the saints, the liturgy, leaders, Scripture, church councils, and sacraments are all channels of the Spirit's presence and the life of the Triune God. The Eastern Church in this way resisted the domestication of the Spirit in the institutional church somewhat more than the Western Church, though it has had its own challenges in this regard—particularly in the form of a diminished sense of the missional call of the Spirit through the church.

With the decay and passing of Christendom, the doctrine of the Spirit has broken out of its limiting institutional containers, as we will see further in Chapter Five. And the Christendom traditions themselves are renewing and recovering a more dynamic doctrine of the Spirit in this new environment.

Radical Traditions

A second and sharply contrasting view of the Spirit emerged among those in the sixteenth century who were called *Radicals*. In the twentieth century, this stream is often called the *Believers Church*. That name became common in the 1960s as a way of identifying "that segment of the Christian heritage which is distinct both from classical Protestantism and from Catholic—Roman, Eastern, and Anglican—understandings of the church."[8] For much of the first two centuries of their existence after their emergence in the 1520s, these Christians were dissenters and outsiders, viewed by the Christian establishment as heretics, schismatics, and rebels against the social order. They came to be called *Anabaptists*.

A key issue for the Anabaptists was the break with Christendom. The church, they thought, must be "free" of the state in order to stand properly apart from the "world" and be a faithful church. Adult baptism (or re-baptism, which is the meaning of ana-baptism) was the symbol of this break with the state church system.

Menno Simons, leader of sixteenth-century Dutch Anabaptism, set out six defining marks of the church. To the two defining Protestant marks (preaching the gospel and rightly observing the sacraments), he added holy living, brotherly and sisterly love, witness (mission), and the cross (suffering).[9] In the twentieth century, Donald Durnbaugh characterized the Believers Church as marked by discipleship, missionary vitality, separation of church and state, mutual aid in community, and a distinctive kind of ecumenicity.[10] For the early Anabaptists, the church was in its very essence a pilgrim and missionary church marked by the way of suffering and martyrdom.

This radical break with Christendom flowed in several streams. Those we could call Spiritualist Anabaptists embraced belief in the Spirit's direct inspiration, thus elevating the Spirit over the Word. This claim could stir up attempts to overthrow the established and corrupt social order. For example, Thomas Müntzer incited the bloody Peasants Revolt in 1524, claiming the Spirit's authority, which drew Martin Luther's scorn, charging that Müntzer had "swallowed the Holy Spirit feathers and all." Other early Radicals like Melchior Hoffman also sought to bypass and undermine the established authority of Christendom by claiming the direct inspiration of the Spirit. This early tendency in Radical Protestantism helped inhibit, among both Catholics and Protestants, renewed and fuller attention to the Spirit.

But the central stream of the Radical Reformation was composed of those we can call Evangelical Anabaptists. For them, the key focus was *discipleship* or actually walking in the way of Jesus; their central image of the church was a "fellowship of the Spirit," where the Christian life is an actually experienced and received reality, and church membership takes place through the fresh reception of the Spirit by each believer. In this view, being a Christian means not simply a formal partaking of the sacraments (where one might remain unformed as a disciple) or claiming to be justified by faith alone (where one might also remain unformed as a disciple), but rather having one's character transformed by the power of the Spirit to be like Jesus and walk in his way.

In the Radical vision, being a Christian involved not just a formal possession of church membership but an actual possession of life in Christ (or in Pauline idiom, "Anyone who does not possess the Spirit of Christ does not belong to Christ"). The gift of God's Spirit is the starting point of Christian life, and this gift is closely related to the practice of believers' baptism. Lesslie Newbigin points out that neither Protestant doctrinal orthodoxy nor Catholic apostolic succession could take the place of the church as a community of the Spirit. This was a dimension significantly diminished in the Christendom traditions, both Catholic and Protestant.[11]

The Radical Christians, especially the early Anabaptists, insisted that no authoritative structure or body of doctrine makes a group an authentic body of Christ. Rather, authentic believers should seek to live as Christ lived. "Most basic in this vision," Harold Bender wrote, "was the conception of the essence of Christianity as discipleship. It meant the transformation of the entire way of life so that it should be fashioned after the teaching and example of Christ. The Anabaptists could not accept a Christianity which made regeneration, holiness, and love primarily a matter of intellect, of doctrinal belief, or of subjective 'experience' rather than one of the transformation of life."[12]

In the Christendom traditions, both Catholic and Protestant, spirituality tended to have an inward focus. The problem for Augustine became disordered desires in one's heart, so an intense emphasis on introspection began to emerge. The same was largely true in Protestantism. The Christian life became more and more a life of interiority. In Christendom, citizenship and church membership were almost synonymous, so there were many church members who had not experienced the new birth and who were not committed to following Jesus.

The Radical vision sought to resist this impulse to turn spirituality primarily into a private inwardness. Among Evangelical Anabaptists, spirituality was more outwardly focused. The problem was not just disordered desires but disordered lives—lives not conformed to the way of Jesus. Thus believers must not only seek to feel kindly toward their neighbors; they must also share with them, serve them, and forgive their wrongdoings.

The Radical tradition focused on the Sermon on the Mount as a guide for basic Christian living, not as a higher ethic for the spiritually elite. If one asks, "How can we actually follow the Sermon on the Mount? It seems impossible!," the Radical would reply, "Yes, such a way is humanly impossible; the Holy Spirit, working through the community of faith, must supernaturally conform our lives to such a way." As John Yoder, the leading advocate of this Radical vision in the twentieth century, put it, "Christian ethics calls for behavior that is impossible except by the miracles of the Holy Spirit."[13]

In the Radical vision, the Spirit is experienced most fully, not mystically or inwardly, but when people serve each other, display the character of Christ, and carry out God's mission in the world. Radical theologians often critiqued the Protestant churches for preaching a "sweet Christ" who required only that one have faith. The Radicals believed that one must yield inwardly to God, experience the new birth, and be remade by the Spirit into a new person. They believed that the believer's inner state of grace would be visible externally in lives conformed to Christ's way. Thus they expected the preaching of the gospel to produce visibly reformed congregations—congregations simply incompatible with those of Christendom.

The Radical traditions tended not only towards steady splintering and disorder but also to downplay the creational breadth of the Spirit's mission. They tended to open a deep divide between human culture and the redeemed community, thereby diminishing a sense of the Spirit's work through nature and culture.

Renewal Traditions

If the Christendom traditions tended to institutionalize the Spirit, renewal traditions tended to privatize the Spirit, focusing on believers' personal relationships with Jesus and on the private experience of renewal through the Spirit. Indeed, one could characterize views of the Spirit in Christian history as swinging back and forth between an institutional focus (as in Christendom traditions, both Catholic and Protestant) and an experiential focus (as in Pietist movements).[14]

The modern Pietist movement began in the seventeenth century as a reaction against (1) Protestant scholasticism, with its perceived spiritual coldness and focus on precision of doctrines, and (2) the widespread nominal Christianity of Christendom. An important forerunner of the movement was *True Christianity* (1605–10) by the Lutheran Johann Arndt; its founding manifesto was the *Pia Desideria* ("Heartfelt Desire for God-Pleasing Reform") by Philipp Jacob Spener, first published in 1675. In the centuries that followed, Pietism became an umbrella term for various movements stressing the centrality of the conversion experience, "vital piety," and the disciplines nurturing one's interior life with God.

With the growing dominance in the eighteenth century of the new secular and scientific worldview brought by the Enlightenment, Pietism tended to compartmentalize the faith in the individual's private and interior life. The new humanistic outlook had little room for a personal God who is present and active in history, so Pietist movements, against the cultural tide, maintained the vibrancy of faith by narrowing its scope to the individual.

The largest and most influential Pietist movement in the eighteenth and nineteenth centuries was John Wesley's "Methodist" revival. Its beginnings are usually dated to his famous Aldersgate experience on May 24, 1738, where he wrote that during the evening's reading of Scripture, he found his heart "strangely warmed." It was not a conversion experience—that had happened in 1725—but it was a turning point for Wesley in his long quest for assurance that his sins were forgiven and for peace with God. For him, it was a powerful experience of the "internal witness of the Holy Spirit" (cf. Rom. 8:10–17 and Eph. 2:8–10), a powerful assurance of God's grace and pardon.

In the years that followed, as a result, Wesley emphasized "the testimony of the Spirit as an inward impression on the soul, whereby the Spirit of God directly 'witnesses to my spirit that I am a child of God.'" But he was careful to correlate the Spirit's inward witness with the Spirit's genuine fruit—that is, what he called "inward and outward holiness." To be born of the Spirit brings a deep change to a person's life: "The [converted person] feels in his heart the mighty working of the Spirit of God; he is inwardly sensible of the graces which the Spirit of God works in his heart. . . . God is continually breathing, as it were, upon his soul and his soul is breathing unto God. Grace is descending into his heart, and prayer and praise ascending to heaven . . . and the child of God grows up, till he comes 'to the full measure of the stature of Christ.'"[15] For Wesley, the experience of the Spirit always joined together inner enjoyment and assurance of God's saving work with outer growth in holiness of life.

The Methodist movement took shape around a system of small groups, called "classes," where members experienced rich fellowship in the Spirit and practiced Bible study, prayer, and rigorous methods of self-examination and accountability. With aggressive itinerant preaching, along with these simple structures, the Methodist movement spread rapidly in England, America, and beyond.

By the 1770s, Wesley believed that the end-time work of the Spirit had begun with the rise of the Methodist movement, and that it would continue to spread throughout the world. In fact, he believed that the Methodist revival in England and America was the first sign that a "New Pentecost" was occurring that would fulfill the original Pentecost world-wide, marked by "inward and outward holiness, or 'righteousness, peace and joy in the Holy Ghost.'"[16] In America between 1776 and 1850, as if to corroborate Wesley's prediction, the Methodist revival experienced a "miracle of growth," from fewer than 3 percent of all church members in 1776 to more than 34 percent by 1850.[17]

The Wesleyan view of the Spirit, along with the theology of the Calvinist Jonathan Edwards, laid the foundation for Protestant revivalism in the late eighteenth and nineteenth centuries. Both men, though differing on key points, insisted that God converted people by the immediate work of the Holy Spirit—that is, by a sovereign divine act not contingent upon any human "means" or efforts (though God might well use such means). Further, both men taught that conversion followed a basic pattern: (1) an initial awakening to one's dangerous and lost spiritual condition; (2) a period of distress and deepening conviction of one's utter helplessness before God; and (3) an experience of deliverance in which the Holy Spirit filled one's heart with love for God and granted assurance of forgiveness.[18] This pattern of conversion was mediated to Presbyterians, Congregationalists, and Baptists; wide use of Wesley's sermons spread it among Methodists. This understanding of the Spirit and conversion became standard in both the First and Second Great Awakenings in America. And it was the basis for the innovation called the "mourner's bench" in the revivals of the nineteenth century.

The impact of Pietism on the Christian faith in the modern world is incalculable. It placed central focus on experience of the Spirit and the practice of spiritual disciplines; it thereby "refreshed (and sometimes splintered) generations of Lutherans, Anglicans, Reformed, Baptists, Methodists, and Adventists. Pietism is, if not the heart of worldwide evangelicalism, certainly one of its chambers."[19] Its weaknesses include its strong individualism, which tended to narrow the scope of mission to saving individual souls and to diminish the creational breadth of salvation, and its elevation of private experience, which tended to depreciate the importance of the church and its sacraments. This was especially true of nineteenth and twentieth century revivalism—less so of the mainstream of the Methodist movement.

Modernist Traditions

Modernist views of the Spirit arose in response to the Enlightenment and the sharp strictures it began to impose on how one determines what is real. Stress fell more and more upon the "reasonableness of Christianity" measured by the new scientific empiricism. A simple typology can provide a handle on modernist views of the Spirit: one type rationalizes the Spirit, virtually collapsing the Spirit into the Word (early modern); another type universalizes the Spirit, untethering the Spirit from the Word (late modern).

Collapsing the Spirit into the Word

The Stone-Campbell movement in the nineteenth century provides an example of the first type. Thomas Campbell and his son Alexander immigrated to America from Ireland in the opening years of the century. They were Presbyterians schooled in the Scottish Philosophy at Glasgow University. Distressed by the fractious denominationalism and overheated revivalism they encountered in America, they sought a simple, rational path to Christian unity. Putting aside the historic creeds and confessions, they proposed what Alexander called "the ancient gospel and order of things" as the basis for unity. That message launched a rapidly growing movement.

Alexander Campbell placed tight strictures on divine agency in the world. God's power to affect people, he said many times, is "all contained in [revealed] words." The Bible already "contains all the arguments which can be offered to reconcile man to God, and to purify them who are reconciled," and therefore "all the power of the Holy Spirit which can operate on the human mind is spent." To be filled with the Spirit thus meant little more than having the words and arguments of the Bible in one's mind. Thus the basic difference between the "natural man" and the "spiritual man" was that the first possessed only the five senses as an avenue to knowledge, while the second possessed the Bible in addition. And in regard to prayer's petitions, one must not expect that "the laws of nature are to be changed, suspended, or new-modified, or that we are to become the subjects of any supernatural aid in obtaining these things." Campbell affirmed divine providence but defined it simply as the "power of circumstances": "no new miracles are wrought, no new laws or impulses are created."[20]

Drawing upon the Lockean or Baconian Philosophy, Campbell asserted that there are two—and only two—types of power that can operate upon human beings: physical power, which operates upon matter, and moral power, which operates upon the mind or will. Moral power consists of arguments or motives. The only way the human spirit can exert power over another spirit is through arguments and motives, all of which are expressed in words. By analogy, the same is true for God's Spirit. "As the spirit of man puts forth all its moral power in the words which it fills with its ideas," Campbell wrote in 1831, "so the Spirit of God puts forth all its converting and sanctifying power in the words which it fills with its ideas." Indeed, it is impossible to imagine that the divine Spirit's influence upon our spirits "can consist in anything else but words and arguments."[21]

An influential book from the early twentieth century shows the enduring nature of this view of the Spirit: the author is Z. T. Sweeney and the title is *The Spirit and the Word*, published in 1919 and reprinted throughout the twentieth century. Sweeney argued that all the work of the Comforter or Paraclete (as stated by Jesus in John 14–16) applied only to the twelve apostles, not to any Christians coming after them. The Spirit as Comforter, he said, was a "private and peculiar" gift to the twelve for their one-time work of establishing the foundations of the church and producing inspired writings. Once this work of the Spirit was completed through the original apostles, "no man has been guided, shown and directed personally by him since." "God does no unnecessary work, and the work of the Paraclete is not necessary now. His work remains [only] in the teachings and lives of the apostles."

Sweeney embraced Campbell's (Lockean) theory that there are only two possible means by which one spirit (or the Holy Spirit) can influence another spirit: (1) physically or "immediately" through the five senses, or (2) rationally or "morally" through words and arguments. After the apostles and the inspiring of the New Testament, God's Spirit no longer works immediately but only as mediated through words and arguments.

This assumption led Sweeney to a remarkable conclusion: scores of the New Testament's statements and admonitions regarding the Spirit simply do not apply to Christians living after the apostles. Here are some examples that Sweeney listed for his readers:

> You were sealed with the Holy Spirit of promise, which is an earnest of our inheritance. (Eph. 1:13, 14)

> [B]e filled with the Spirit . . . (Eph. 5:18)

> He saved us through the washing of regeneration and the renewing of the Holy Spirit . . . (Titus 3:5)

> He has given us of his Spirit. (1 John 4:13)

Sweeney insisted that all of these verses, and a long list of others, apply only to first-century believers in whom God was "manifesting his presence by supernatural demonstrations"; but now that God works only through the words of Scripture, all these texts "lack meaning" for Christians since that era.[22]

This "Word only" view of the Spirit, also set forth by Alexander Campbell, became prominent in the Stone-Campbell tradition, especially among the branch known as Churches of Christ.[23] The tradition combined an ardent attempt to "restore" earliest Christianity with a thoroughly (early) modern view of the Spirit. Other biblicist traditions have not made this exact argument but functionally have also collapsed the Spirit into the Word.

If this nineteenth-century view rationalized the Spirit, virtually collapsing the Spirit into the Word, twentieth-century modernist views moved toward universalizing the Spirit, untethering the Spirit from the Word.

Universalizing the Spirit

In contrast to the long-dominant mainstream of Christian history that has confessed Jesus as the one Lord and Savior of the world, the twentieth-century modernist tradition rejected a "Christocentric universalism" in favor of what we could call a "Spirit universalism." A main driving force of this move was the engagement with other religions. Liberal advocates of religious pluralism wanted to affirm that God can be truly known through many different religious traditions. Religious pluralists prefer to treat Jesus as the agent through whom God is revealed to Christians, and the Spirit as the agent through whom God is revealed in other religious. "The Spirit then becomes the god present in all the world's spiritualities, whose divine work there need have no coherence with the work of Jesus Christ."[24]

Since about 1968, the World Council of Churches has tended to pursue this strategy. In the period surrounding the Canberra (Australia) assembly in 1991, where the theme was "Come Holy Spirit, Renew the Whole Creation," this position became clearly dominant. "Without being in God, one cannot produce the fruits of the Spirit of God. For Christians to be in Christ is indeed to be in God. But in a religiously plural world, to be in Christ is not the only way to be in God."[25]

Though dominated by more liberal views of the Spirit, the final reports contained strong dissent by the Orthodox churches and Evangelicals. The Orthodox stressed the imperative to "guard against a tendency *to substitute a 'private' spirit, or a spirit of the world, or other spirits for the Holy Spirit*" (italics original). The Evangelicals urged that "Spirits must be discerned. Not every spirit is of the Holy Spirit. The primary criterion for discerning the Holy Spirit is that the Holy Spirit is the Spirit of Christ. The Holy Spirit points to the cross and resurrection and witnesses to the Lordship of Christ."[26]

There are numerous variations on this late modernist view of the Spirit. One variation denies both the distinct personhood of the Spirit and Jesus as the incarnate Word. Spirit becomes a symbol denoting not a distinct third person of the Trinity, but the way God reaches out to human beings. In this view, God encounters people directly, and this direct encounter makes unnecessary a mediator—the incarnate Word—who works atonement between God and humanity. *Spirit* thus refers to the immediate experience of God in the here and now, and Jesus is viewed as a human being who, because of the unqualified presence of God in his life, lived in full obedience and selfless love. He was the perfect model of the presence of God as spirit in a human life. And his example can inspire in us a similar—though imperfect—response to God so that we, like Jesus, become children of God. Another variation moves toward pantheism. Through the Spirit, God "enters into relationship with the world, making it God's own 'body.'"[27]

A basic weakness of this second type of modernist view of the Spirit is that, in separating the Spirit from Christ, the Spirit gets easily tied to a broad array of ideologies and social causes, and separated from the Spirit's intimate relation to and focus on Jesus the Son. The modernist traditions, in general, moved beyond the sphere of Christian orthodoxy.

Pentecostal/Charismatic Traditions

The explosive global growth of Pentecostalism (in its myriad forms) in the twentieth century has been a key force bringing new attention to the doctrine of the Spirit. Donald Dayton calls Pentecostalism "a corrective to the classical traditions of Christian faith."[28] It represents a major break with the constricted Western worldview that emerged with the Enlightenment. And it was a protest and reaction against the nominal Christianity that had come down from Christendom and did not reflect the powerful conversions that seemed normal in the New Testament, evidencing a deeply tamed understanding of God's mission in the world.

We can say that the modern Pentecostal movement in our time, especially in the Global South, is similar to what the Anabaptist movement was to the sixteenth century. As John Yoder observed, "The Pentecostal movement is in our century the closest parallel to what Anabaptism was in the sixteenth century: expanding so vigorously that it bursts the bonds of its own thinking about church order, living from the multiple gifts of the Spirit in the total church . . . unembarrassed by the language of the layman and the aesthetic tastes of the poor." And missiologist Andrew

Wall has characterized the Pentecostal African Independent Churches as the "Anabaptists of Africa."[29]

The modern Pentecostal movement is normally dated from a series of meetings led by William Seymour in Azusa Street, Los Angeles, that began in 1906. But its beginnings can be traced back a little earlier, to Charles Parham at Topeka Bible College in Kansas, when in 1900 the distinctive Pentecostal teaching—that tongues speech was the sign of Spirit baptism—was first fully set forth.

The roots of early Pentecostalism lie in the Methodist movement and in the nineteenth-century Holiness movement. Both movements claimed that the Christian life is experienced in two stages: first, in the experience of conversion to Christ, and second, in a later distinct experience of the Spirit. For Wesley, the second stage was the experience of "entire sanctification"—that is, a state in which one did not consciously commit sin; for the Holiness movement, which arose mostly out of Methodism, it was an instantaneous, supernatural work of perfecting grace.[30] Shaped by this tradition, the early Pentecostals interpreted Acts 1:8, "when the Holy Spirit has come upon you," as a second experience of the Spirit subsequent to conversion, often called "the second blessing." But they went a step further, believing that the "initial evidence" of this second blessing or Spirit baptism was provided by the gift of tongues speech. This view became standard in what can be called the classical Pentecostal tradition.[31]

Some historians speak of three "waves" of the Spirit in the twentieth century, with Pentecostalism being the first. The second "wave" of the Spirit emerged in the Charismatic renewal of the late 1950s and 1960s that spread throughout most of the historic Christian traditions, including the Roman Catholic, beginning in 1967. It is often called the Charismatic movement; in Britain and Europe, it was called simply the Renewal movement. The Charismatic movement rejected the Pentecostal doctrine of baptism in the Spirit as a second work of grace manifested by tongues speech, but it generally accepted the full range of New Testament "gifts of the Spirit." "The majority of denominations adopted positions of cautious openness, neither welcoming C.R. [Charismatic Renewal] with enthusiasm, nor rejecting it as inauthentic."[32] Pope Paul VI called the widespread Catholic Charismatic movement a gift to the church.

The "third wave" of the renewal movement, as Peter Wagner called it, emerged in the 1980s and is sometimes called "neo-Charismatic." It stressed the inbreaking kingdom of God, healing as a sign of the kingdom, the casting out of demons, and the gift of prophecy. The movement was open to all the gifts of the Spirit, but viewed baptism in the Spirit not as a "second blessing" but as occurring at conversion (1 Cor. 12:13); it spoke of repeated fillings with the Spirit and viewed tongues-speech as one gift among others, not as "initial evidence" of Spirit baptism.

Prominent in this "third wave" movement in the West are the large networks of churches associated with Calvary Chapel, Vineyard Christian Fellowship, and Hope Chapel, as well as many independent churches. Sociologist Donald Miller called them "new paradigm churches" because they broke sharply with the long-dominant Western worldview and looked to first-century Christianity for "a radical spirituality that undermines the cynicism and fragmentation" of postmodern culture. "New paradigm Christians are quite comfortable," said Miller, "with an epistemology that . . . interjects God into everyday experience, denying the sacred-profane split" that became the norm in the modern West.[33]

Recent statistics estimate that there are 612 million Pentecostal, Charismatic, and neo-Charismatic believers in the world—an astonishing number. The neo-Charismatic label is used as an enormous "catch-all" category of independent churches and movements that, though differing from classic Pentecostalism, all share an emphasis on the gifts of the Spirit and "a desire to receive more of God's empowering for the Christian life." These groups include the Han Chinese Independent Churches (estimated at 80 million) and the African Independent Churches (with 55 million).[34]

After the explosive growth of Christianity in the Global South, it is estimated that Pentecostal/Charismatic movements, in their wide diversity, make up 25 to 30 percent of all professed Christians in the world. Among the more than one billion Roman Catholics around the world, about 25 percent (250 million) can be considered Charismatic in orientation, with most of them in the Global South.[35] Both the historic and the indigenous churches around the world, especially in the Global South, are more and more dominated by Charismatic forms of Christian faith. "With only some hyperbole, we might say that although some of the world's new Christian communities are Roman Catholic, some Anglican, some Baptist, some Presbyterian and many independent, almost all are Pentecostal in a broad sense of the term."[36]

The wide diversity of these movements makes them difficult to classify, but one observer proposes this minimalist definition: "Segments of Christianity that believe and experience the dynamic work of the Holy Spirit, including supernatural demonstrations of God's power and spiritual gifts, with consequent dynamic and participatory worship and zeal for evangelism."[37]

The Pentecostal/Charismatic traditions, of course, have not lacked for critics. One theologian, a Pentecostal himself, critiques the tendency to downplay doctrine and the "elitist assumptions of Pentecostal revivalism," and he deplores the way that global Pentecostalism has become "a disconnected cafeteria of ideas."[38] Yves Congar, a Roman Catholic sympathetic to the renewal movements, raised several common concerns about these movements. One was a concern about the primary focus on the immediacy of the Spirit, a focus that easily pushes to the side the traditional spiritual disciplines, including Scripture study, as an important means of growth. Another concern was the superficiality of some charismatic spirituality. Congar pointed out that spiritual writers in the Christian tradition warned about seeking dramatic experiences of the Spirit since, if they are genuine, one's responsibilities also greatly increase; the experience of God is an awesome thing, often leading one into deep sacrifice and arduous service.[39]

Looking over these five streams or traditions, we can see that views of the Spirit in Christian history have tended to swing back and forth between an institutional focus (as in Christendom traditions) and an experiential focus (as in Pietism, Revivalism, and Pentecostalism). Often missing or downplayed in both is the eschatological dynamism associated with the presence of the Spirit in the New Testament. I would quickly add that the

Spirit transcends the limits of each cluster of traditions and continues to carry forward God's mission to bring about the restoration of all things through the Son.

This brief tracing of five types of Spirit traditions is meant to provide a historical framework, a broader horizon, in which to consider a robust doctrine of the Spirit today—one rooted in Scripture, shaped by wisdom from the tradition, and focused on the mission of God.

NOTES

[1] Augustine, *On the Trinity* 15.17.27.

[2] Augustine, *On Baptism* 3.16.21.

[3] Colin Gunton, *The Promise of Trinitarian Theology* (Edinburgh, Scotland: T & T Clark, 1991), 51.

[4] James D. G. Dunn, *Baptism in the Holy Spirit* (Naperville, IL: Allenson, 1970), 225.

[5] Kilian McDonnell, "The Determinative Doctrine of the Holy Spirit," *Theology Today* 39 (1982): 142.

[6] Timothy Ware, *The Orthodox Church* (London: Penguin, 1963), 222.

[7] Dumitru Staniloae, *The Experience of God*, trans. Ioan Ionita and Robert Barringer (Brookline, MA: Holy Cross, 1994), 55; George Florovsky, *Bible, Church, Tradition: An Eastern Orthodox View* (Belmont, MA: Nordland 1972), 46–47.

[8] James Leo Garrett, Jr., "Preface," *The Concept of the Believers' Church* (Scottdale, PA: Herald, 1968), 5.

[9] *Complete Writings of Menno Simons, 1496–1561*, trans. Leonard Verduin and ed. John Wenger (Scottdale, PA: Herald, 1956), 739–44.

[10] Donald Durnbaugh, *The Believers' Church: The History and Character of Radical Protestantism* (1968; Scottdale, PA: Herald Press, 1985), 209–99.

[11] Lesslie Newbigin, *The Household of God: Lectures on the Nature of the Church* (New York: Friendship, 1954).

[12] Harold Bender, "The Anabaptist Vision," *Church History* 13, no. 1 (1944): 3–24.

[13] John H. Yoder, "Let the Church Be the Church," *The Royal Priesthood: Essays Ecclesiological and Ecumenical* (Grand Rapids: Eerdmans, 1994), 174.

[14] See David Beck, *The Holy Spirit and the Renewal of All Things* (Eugene, OR: Pickwick, 2007), 1–14.

[15] John Wesley, "The Witness of the Spirit" (1746); Sermon 45, "The New Birth," II, 4–5. See Winfield H. Bevins, "The Historical Development of Wesley's Doctrine of the Spirit," *Wesleyan Theological Journal* 41, no. 2 (fall 2006): 161–81.

[16] John Wesley, *The Works of John Wesley*, 3rd edition (Grand Rapids: Baker, 1996), 6:308.

[17] Roger Finke and Rodney Stark, "How the Upstart Sects Won America: 1776–1850," *Journal for the Scientific Study of Religion* 28, no. 1 (1988): 27–44.

[18] See Jonathan Edwards, *Religious Affections* (New Haven, CT: Yale University, 1959), 197–239, and John Wesley, *Fifty-Three Sermons*, ed. Edward H. Sugden (Nashville, TN: Abingdon, 1984).

[19] Telford Work, "Pneumatology," in *Mapping Modern Theology: A Thematic and Historical Introduction*, ed. Kelly M. Kapic and Bruce L. McCormack (Grand Rapids: Baker Academic, 2012), 233.

[20] Alexander Campbell, "Dialogue on the Holy Spirit—Part 1," *Millennial Harbinger* 2 (July 4, 1831): 295, 296; "Dialogue on the Holy Spirit—Part 2," *Millennial Harbinger* 2 (August 1831): 369; "Incidents on a Tour to Nashville, TN. No. 1," *Millennial Harbinger* 1 (December 6, 1830): 560; "Prayer—No. 1," *Millennial Harbinger* 2 (October 1831):

471; "Mr. Lynd on the Influence of the Holy Spirit," *Millennial Harbinger* new ser. 1 (September 1837): 409.

[21] Alexander Campbell, "The Whole Work of the Holy Spirit in the Salvation of Men," *Millennial Harbinger* 2 (July 1831): 293–95; see also Campbell, "Mr. Lynd on the Influence of the Holy Spirit," 408.

[22] Z. T. Sweeney, *The Spirit and the Word: A Treatise on the Holy Spirit in Light of a Rational Interpretation of the Word of Truth* (1919; reprint ed., Nashville, TN: Gospel Advocate, 1950), 67–79, 95–97, 99.

[23] For this story, see Leonard Allen, "Unearthing the 'Dirt Philosophy': Faith and the Quenching of the Spirit," in *Things Unseen: Churches of Christ in (and after) the Modern Age* (Abilene, TX: Leafwood Publishers, 2004), 71–98.

[24] Work, "Pneumatology," 247.

[25] Stanley J. Samartha, "The Holy Spirit and People of Other Faiths," in *To the Wind of God's Spirit: Reflections on the Canberra Theme* (Geneva: WCC, 1990), 59.

[26] *Signs of the Spirit: Official Report of the Seventh Assembly of the WCC, Canberra, 1991*, ed. Michael Kinnamon (Geneva: WCC, 1991), 279, 282.

[27] Geoffrey Lampe, *God as Spirit* (Oxford: Clarendon Press, 1977), 23–25, 37; Peter C. Hodgson, *Winds of the Spirit: A Constructive Christian Theology* (Philadelphia: Westminster John Knox, 1994), 163f.

[28] Donald Dayton, "The Holy Spirit and Christian Expansion in the Twentieth Century," *Missiology* 16, no. 4 (1988): 402.

[29] John Yoder, quoted by Roelf Kuitse, "Holy Spirit: Source of Messianic Mission," in *The Transfiguration of Mission: Biblical, Theological, and Historical Foundations* (1993; Eugene, OR: Wipf & Stock, 2007), 108; Andrew Walls, "The Challenge of the African Independent Churches: The Anabaptists of Africa?" in *The Missionary Movement in Christian History: Studies in the Transmission of Faith* (Maryknoll, NY: Orbis, 1996), 111–19.

[30] Donald Dayton, *Theological Roots of Pentecostalism* (Peabody, MA: Hendrickson, 1987), 35–80.

[31] See Gary McGee, ed., *Initial Evidence: Historical and Biblical Perspective on the Pentecostal Doctrine of Spirit Baptism* (Eugene, OR: Wipf & Stock, 1991), 41–95.

[32] Peter Hocken, "Charismatic Movement," *New International Dictionary of Pentecostal and Charismatic Movements*, ed. Stanley Burgess and Eduard van der Maas (Grand Rapids: Zondervan, 2002).

[33] Donald E. Miller, *Reinventing American Protestantism: Christianity in the New Millennium* (Berkeley, CA: University of California, 1997), 25, 125.

[34] Todd M. Johnson, David B. Barrett, and Peter F. Crossing, "Status of Global Mission, 2012, in the Context of AD 1800–2015," *International Bulletin of Missionary Research* 36 (2012): 29.

[35] Edward Cleary, *The Rise of Charismatic Catholicism in Latin America* (Gainesville: University of Florida, 2011).

[36] Mark Noll, *The New Shape of World Christianity* (Downers Grove, IL: InterVarsity Academic, 2009), 34.

[37] Wonsuk Ma, "'When the Poor Are Fired Up': The Role of Pneumatology in Pentecostal/Charismatic Mission," in *Spirit in the World: Emerging Pentecostal Theologies in Global Contexts*, ed. Veli-Matti Karkkainen (Grand Rapids: Eerdmans, 2009), 41.

[38] Frank Macchia, *Baptized in the Spirit: A Global Pentecostal Theology* (Grand Rapids: Zondervan, 2006), 113, 27.

[39] Yves Congar, *I Believe in the Holy Spirit* (London: Geoffrey Chapman, 1983), 2:165ff.

3

TRINITY

The Spirit is fully God and shares the rich life of the Father and the Son; this focus provides a check against distortions and deficiencies in the Body of Christ.

Father, Son and Holy Spirit are to be known only in a perfect Trinity, in closest interaction and unity, before all creation.
—Gregory of Nyssa

We believe in the Holy Spirit, the Lord and Giver of Life who proceeds from the Father, who with the Father and the Son is worshipped and glorified, who spoke through the prophets.
—Nicene Creed

Recovery of a practical faith in the power of the Holy Spirit will lead us astray if it is not held firmly with an equally practical Trinitarian faith.
—Lesslie Newbigin

The New Testament's account of the work of the Spirit presupposes, indeed requires, a Trinitarian understanding of God. Our understanding of the Spirit must be rooted in the biblical revelation of God as Triune—that is, as three distinct persons who in perfect relationship make up one God. The renewal of the doctrine of the Trinity in the twentieth century has set the stage for this important grounding.

The Revelation of God as Triune

Though the word *trinity* is not a biblical word, a threefold pattern of divine relationality permeates the New Testament. There is a deep, almost unreflective recognition of the diversity and unity of God by the New Testament writers, and their language about this relationality becomes the raw material for what later became Trinitarian orthodoxy. As Gordon Fee puts it, "Paul affirms, asserts, and presupposes the Trinity in every way; and those affirmations . . . are precisely the reason the later church took up the question of how."[1]

In Paul's writings, this threefold pattern can be demonstrated from two sets of texts: several that are explicitly Trinitarian, and many more focusing on "salvation in Christ" that are less explicit but with a clear Trinitarian pattern. One explicit text is 1 Corinthians 12:4–6, where Paul correlates the gifts and working of the Spirit, the Lord Jesus, and God. He points to "different kinds of gifts, but the same Spirit," "different kinds of service, but the same Lord," and "different kinds of working but in all of them and in everyone it is the same God at work." Here the apostle assumes, almost unreflectively, that the one God works as a Triune reality.

Another explicit Trinitarian text is the benediction in 2 Corinthians 13:14: "May the grace of the Lord Jesus Christ, and the love of God, and the fellowship of the Holy Spirit be with you all." Here Paul makes a fundamental distinction between the activity of the Father, Son, and Spirit, yet stating in shorthand the basic message of his letters that salvation is the joint working of one God—Father, Son, and Spirit.

A third explicit text is Ephesians 4:4–6, which affirms "one body and one Spirit," "one Lord, one faith, one baptism; one God and Father of all." Here is a kind of early creedal formulation clearly distinguishing the activities of the Triune God. The last phrase—the Father "who is above all and through all and in all"—subordinates the Son and Spirit to the Father (in function not in personhood), but the passage clearly affirms the oneness of the Triune God.

A fourth text, Romans 8:9–11, gives us a rich and important witness to the threefold pattern in the New Testament. Robert Jenson calls Romans 8 the "most remarkable trinitarian passage in the New Testament," with verse 11 providing the heart of the argument:[2] "And if the Spirit of him who raised Jesus from the dead is living in you, he who raised Christ from the dead will also give life to your mortal bodies because of his Spirit who lives in you." How many characters are named here? There is Jesus, there is the one who raised Jesus from the dead, and there is the Spirit of him who raised Jesus. We see three actors, and the text is richly textured in naming these three. All three persons are involved in the resurrection, which comes about through a complex interrelation among them. This interrelation is then extended to include human beings who will "also" be raised from the dead. As a result, "the human person becomes an additional sharer in the life that the Father through the Spirit shares with Christ."[3]

Many other Pauline texts, especially those that lay out his formulation of the gospel, demonstrate the threefold pattern of divine relationality. Romans 5:1–8 is a rich one. Because of God's love, "Christ died for the ungodly," and through him we have "peace with God" and "hope of sharing the glory of God"; furthermore, we experience God's love because it has been "poured into our hearts through the Holy Spirit who has been given to us" (ESV).

Another text is Galatians 4:4–6, which affirms that because we have been adopted as sons, "God has sent the Spirit of his Son into our hearts, crying, 'Abba, Father!'" And another is 2 Corinthians 1:20–22, where God has affirmed us through Christ—God's "Yes"—and "put his Spirit in our hearts as a deposit, [or down payment] guaranteeing our inheritance." Many other texts portray salvation as the threefold work of the one God (see, for example, 1 Thess. 1:4–5; 2 Thess. 2:13–14; 1 Cor. 2:4–5; 6:19–20; Gal. 3:1–5; Eph. 2:20–22; Col. 3:16).

Paul never viewed his conversion as a rejection of his monotheistic Jewish heritage, and never downplayed the ancient revelation of the one God of Israel. Paul assumes that everyone will agree that "God is one" (Rom. 3:30; see also 1 Cor. 8:6; Eph. 4:6; 1 Tim. 2:5). In short, Paul remained an ardent monotheist; yet because of his encounter with the risen Christ and his experience of the Spirit, he came to know God as a unity of three deeply related persons.

Texts outside of Paul that link Father, Son, and Spirit as a triad include the great commission, where believers are to be baptized in the name of the Father, Son, and Holy Spirit (Matt. 28:19–20). Listing of the Spirit on equal terms with the Father and the Son here indicates the Spirit's distinct personhood. As John Meier commented, "One does not baptize people in the name of a divine person, a holy creature, and an impersonal divine force."[4] And Peter on Pentecost proclaimed, "Exalted to the right hand of God, he [Jesus] has received from the Father the promised Holy Spirit, and has poured out what you now see and hear" (Acts 2:32–33). And the first epistle of Peter is addressed "[To the] exiles . . . who have been chosen according to the foreknowledge of God the Father, through the sanctifying work of the Spirit to be obedient to Jesus Christ and sprinkled with his blood" (1 Pet. 1:2).

In the Gospel of John, we find a particularly rich glimpse into God's relationality. It is not just a matter of pointing to texts that identify the divinity of Jesus or of the Spirit, but rather "identifying the Trinitarian logic that underlies the Johannine text as a whole and at every point."[5] From this Trinitarian logic, one can show how the person of Christ, the work of the Spirit, and the nature of the Christian community are grounded in that logic.

In John's Paraclete discourses, we see a deep intimacy between Jesus, the Father, and the Spirit. Jesus prays to the Father for "those who will believe in me through their message, that all of them may be one, Father, just as you are in me and I am in you. May they also be in us." (John 17:20–21; cf. 14:10–11, 20). Here the Son is "in" the Father, and at the same time, the Father is "in" the Son. The unity of the Father and the Son does not dissolve the distinction between them. In the same context, Jesus says to the disciples, "I will not leave you as orphans; I will come to you" (14:18), but this coming actually turns out to be "the Advocate, the Holy Spirit, whom the Father will send in my name" (14:26). Indeed, it is good for Jesus to go away so that the Advocate can come. And when the Spirit comes, the Spirit will testify about Christ, making known to them only what the Spirit receives from Christ (15:7, 26; 16:13–15).

Here I pause to consider a later development based on John's rich language: By the latter fourth century, there was widespread agreement among Christian leaders that God's nature was properly thought of as a communion of persons. And they began to use the term *perichoresis*, meaning mutual indwelling or mutual submission or dynamic intermingling, to describe this communion. John's language of the Son being "in" the Father and the Father "in" the Son provided the scriptural basis for it. *Perichoresis* described the deep mutual love shared in the life of God between Father, Spirit, and Son. Occasionally the image of a divine dance was used to portray the movement, joy, and perfect love in the life of the Trinity.

The modern guild of biblical scholars has tended to view talk about "trinity" in the New Testament as anachronistic, as a construct from a later time imposed back upon Scripture. Against this strong tendency, Francis Watson asserts that "the triadic pattern exemplified by 2 Corinthians 13:14 is almost everywhere in the background [of the New Testament], if not in the foreground."[6] And several important recent studies have supported this assertion, showing the deeply relational—indeed "trinitarian"—character of the Father, the Son, and the Spirit in the New Testament.[7]

The explicit doctrine of the Trinity that gradually emerged in the first four centuries was not simply a philosophical construct imposed back upon Scripture but rather a result of the necessary work of filling out the New Testament's pervasive triadic language about God as the gospel mission engaged Greco-Roman culture. Trinitarian reflection was deeply grounded in the missionary encounter with paganism. As missionaries and evangelists proclaimed Jesus, they were faced with the question, "But who is Jesus?" To answer that question, the church "very soon found itself compelled to articulate a fully Trinitarian doctrine of the God whom it proclaimed."[8] The developing doctrine of the Trinity was always rooted in the early Christians' reflection on the Scriptures of Israel and on what God was doing in Jesus Christ, in light of their own encounter with the gospel.[9]

God the Father reaches out through the Son, in the power of Spirit, to touch and transform the creation. God extends the divine life to the church and the creation in the two missions of the Spirit and the Son. In Irenaeus's striking image, the Son and the Spirit are the two hands of God to open the way back to the Father, who is the source of all. Very early in the Christian movement (later second century), Irenaeus clearly stated this Trinitarian dynamic: "Such is the rhythm, such is the movement through which the human person, created and modeled, becomes the image and the resemblance of the uncreated God. The Father decides and commands, the Son executes and models, the Spirit nourishes and grows."[10]

A fundamental Christian confession is that God is one. For this reason, the classic doctrine of the Trinity has insisted that the actions of the Trinity on behalf of the world are indivisible. This has been a basic guiding "rule" in setting forth the doctrine. So the identity and work of the Son should not be understood apart from the Spirit, and the identity and work of the Spirit not apart from the Son. Father, Son, and Spirit share a deep oneness that is constituted by love and by the gifts each gives the other. They share one will and purpose. The widespread view that creation is the work of the Father, redemption is the work of the Son, and sanctification is the work of the Spirit does not properly uphold that essential oneness. The Father does not act on his own apart from the Son, and the Son doesn't act on his own without the Spirit. "Every operation which extends from God to creation ... has its origin in the Father, proceeds through the Son, and reaches its completion by the Holy Spirit."[11]

Father, Son, and Spirit always operate in unity though each person in a different manner. Thus we can distinguish the roles of Father, Son, and Spirit as we see their interactions revealed in Scripture. That, after all, is why the Christian faith is Trinitarian at its very core, for that is how Scripture has revealed God's activity to us. So, the next question is, "How do we learn who the Holy Spirit is?"

The Spirit in the Trinity

The backdrop to identifying the Spirit in the New Testament is provided by the main metaphors for the Spirit in the Old Testament. Wind or breath is the most prominent, but there are several others: a warming or even a raging fire ("[H]e will cleanse the bloodstains from Jerusalem by a spirit of judgment and a spirit of fire" [Isa. 4:4]); oil, as in anointing ("The Spirit of the Sovereign LORD is on me because the LORD has anointed me" [Isa. 61:1]); running water ("I will pour water on the thirsty land, and streams on the dry ground; I will pour out my Spirit on your offspring, and my blessing on your descendants" [Isa. 44:3]); and wings in flight ("[A]nd the Spirit of God was hovering over the waters" [Gen. 1:1]).

Spirit of God (*ruach*—breath or wind) is often used in the Old Testament to express the mysterious action of God in human life and in creation. To call God "spirit" was to speak of God as a living presence—experienced with two kinds of "breath": a gentle breath moving deeply within a person or a strong wind drawing people into its path.[12] Neither aspect was under human control. Both aspects appear in Ezekiel's vision of the valley of dry bones (Ezek. 37). Israel in exile has lost everything, including, they seem to believe, their God; they are like a heap of dry bones bleaching in the desert sun. Yahweh promises to come like the wind (which can be translated wind, breath, or spirit; Ezek. 37:9). God will breathe and the four winds of the earth will blow, giving the people life and causing them to stand on their feet in formation like an army ready for action.

As Israel's prophets envisioned the age to come, they looked for a much richer experience of God's powerful presence within Israel (Ezek. 36:26–27, 39:29; 37; Isa. 44:3; Joel 2:28–29). Alongside this expectation was the expectation of a Spirit-anointed person (Messiah): "the Spirit of the LORD will rest on him—the Spirit of wisdom and of understanding" (Isa. 11:2); "the spirit of the Sovereign LORD is on me, because the LORD has anointed me to proclaim good news to the poor" (Isa. 61:1).

These nonpersonal metaphors, along with the expectation of a Spirit-anointed person, come to a personal focus in the New Testament with the coming of Christ. At Mary's conception of Jesus, the Spirit came upon her and "*overshadowed*" her (recalling the Genesis creation story). Jesus was *anointed* with the Spirit at his baptism when the Spirit as a *dove* descended and remained on him. Jesus gives the Spirit to his disciples as he *breathed* upon them (John 2:22), and on the day of Pentecost, the disciples experienced the Spirit like a mighty *wind* and tongues of *fire* (Acts 2:2–3). And Paul speaks of being immersed in the Spirit in the *waters* of baptism: "For in the one Spirit we were all baptized into one body" (1 Cor. 12:13 ESV).

We may be tempted to view the Spirit of God as an impersonal power or as the influence of the Creator God in our world. The nonpersonal images noted above—wind, fire, water, oil, and bird—can take us in that direction. In fact, people commonly refer to the Spirit as "it."

But the New Testament speaks of the Spirit using many different verbs that demand a personal agent. For example, the Spirit "testifies" with our spirits that we are children of God (Rom. 8:16), comes alongside to help, and "intercedes" with the Father on our behalf (and God "knows the mind of the Spirit" [Rom. 8:27]). The Spirit "searches" and understands (1 Cor. 2:10–11), distributes gift as the Spirit wills (1 Cor. 12:11), can be "outraged" by rejection (Heb. 10:29, ESV), forbids (Acts 16:6), prevents (Acts 16:7), sends (Acts 13:4), is put to the test (Acts 5:9), and is grieved by our sins (Eph. 4:30). The fullest portrayal of the personhood of the Spirit is found in the Paraclete passages in John 14–16, where the Spirit mediates the Father and the Son to the disciples (especially 14:6–11).[13]

But the Spirit of course is not a person in the same sense that human beings are persons. The New Testament's personal language is sometimes qualified by the nonpersonal images (wind, John 3:8; water, John 7:37–38; fire, Acts 2), thereby helping ensure that we do not confuse the Spirit's personhood with human personhood. It might be better to call the Spirit supra-personal or more-than-personal.

Clearly the New Testament portrays the Spirit acting toward us in a personal way. But is the Spirit a distinct and personal subject within the life of God?

Let's answer that question by examining the New Testament stories of the Spirit's interaction with Jesus. "If even a human person is known not by conceptual analysis, but by narrative," Eugene Rogers asks, "is it to be expected that we would get to know the Spirit in any other way than by her interactions with other persons?"[14] If a person is best identified by narrative, then the distinct personhood of the Spirit can be opened up to us by the New Testament narratives that portray Jesus and the Spirit interacting in the presence of the Father. It was these narratives that pro-ceeded—and helped give rise to—the later doctrinal accounts of the Trinity and of the Spirit.

We can see this narrative identification of the Spirit in the early theo-logians. Here is a well-known passage from Gregory of Nazianzus in the fourth century: "Christ is born, the Spirit is his Forerunner (Lk. 1:35); Christ is baptized, the Spirit bears witness (Lk. 3:21–22); Christ is tempted, the Spirit leads him up (Lk. 4:2, 14); Christ works miracles, the Spirit accompanies him (Matt. 12:22, 28); Christ ascends, the Spirit takes his place (Acts 1:8–9)."[15]

What does the gospel story tells us about how the Spirit functions in the relationship of the Father with his incarnate Son? There we find three main phases of the imparting of the Spirit to Jesus.

First, the Spirit comes to impart human life to Jesus at his conception in the womb of Mary. The angel Gabriel tells Mary that she will conceive and give birth to a son, Jesus. When Mary asks how this can be, the angel says, "The Holy Spirit will come on you, and the power of the Most High will overshadow you. So the holy one to be born will be called the Son of God" (Lk. 1:35). We might say that the Spirit's work here is *regenerative*, not simply generative. The Spirit regenerates the humanity that came from Mary, enabling it to be united in one person with the eternal Son of God. Though Luke's account does not speak of the Son's eternal pre-existence (as does John's), it is clear that this child was not an ordinary human who at some point later in his life becomes the divine Son. The Spirit of God intervenes in the process of human conception to begin a new humanity in the conception of the Son. The conception and birth of Christ was a gift of the Spirit.

Second, at Jesus' baptism in the Jordan, the Spirit rests upon Jesus as a sign of the Father's love and Jesus' anointing as Messiah. As Jesus came out of the water, "heaven was opened and the Holy Spirit descended on him in bodily form like a dove. And a voice came from heaven: 'You are my Son, whom I love; with you I am well pleased'" (Lk. 3:21–22, with a strong allusion to Ps. 2:7). Here Jesus is announced as the Son who receives the Spirit from his Father and also the one who will bestow the Spirit upon his followers. As John the Baptist says, "He will baptize you with the Holy Spirit and fire" (Lk. 3:16). John's account says, "I saw the Spirit come down from heaven as a dove and remain on him" (John 1:32). The verb John uses, translated "remain" or "rest," originates with the Greek (LXX) rendering of Isaiah 11:2, "And the Spirit of the LORD will rest upon him."[16] John's statement that the Spirit remained on him suggests that Jesus here entered a new dimension of his relationship with the Spirit, and a new stage in his life and ministry. It was through this anointing by the Spirit that Jesus, the eternal Son of God, became the "Christ" (anointed one) and received empowerment for his messianic mission.

Full of the Spirit and led by the Spirit into the desert, Jesus was tempted for forty days (Lk. 4:1). He depended on the Spirit to face Satan's temptations and reject the path of worldly power (4:3–9). And the testing or temptation was not limited to the wilderness: Luke says Satan left him only "until an opportune time." The Spirit's empowerment was constant, so that Jesus, filled with the power of the Spirit, returned to Galilee (4:13–14). There he inaugurated his messianic mission with his first sermon: "The Spirit of the Lord is upon me, because he has anointed me to bring good news to the poor, . . . freedom for the prisoners, . . . the year of the Lord's favor" (4:18–19, quoting Isa. 61:1). And under the anointing of the Spirit, Jesus "went around doing good and healing all who were under the power of the devil" (Acts 10:38).

Jürgen Moltmann suggests adding these words to the second article of the Nicene Creed to highlight Christ's anointing by the Spirit:

> Baptized by John the Baptist,
> filled with the Holy Spirit:
> to preach the kingdom of God to the poor,
> to heal the sick,
> to receive those who have been cast out,
> to revive Israel for the salvation of the nations, and
> to have mercy upon all people. [17]

Third, the Spirit transfigures and exalts the risen but still human Jesus Christ. Jesus "through the Spirit of holiness was appointed the Son of God in power by his resurrection from the dead" (Rom. 1:4). Jesus was exalted in a transformed, resurrected humanity by a new work of the Spirit in him. The "last Adam"—the ultimate human—was exalted or transfigured by the Spirit so he could fulfill the Father's purpose for the human race (1 Cor. 15:45, "The last Adam became a life-giving spirit"). From this exalted position, Christ then pours out the Spirit at Pentecost, marking the first installment of our resurrected and transfigured humanity (Acts 2:33).

In these "trinitarian" narratives, Scripture reveals the person of the Spirit in an intimate relationship with Jesus. The Son and the Spirit are interdependent persons who together, in the intimacy of their relationship, work to bring us into the fullness of life the Father desires for us.

The Person without a Face

In the Trinitarian relationality, the Spirit is not inferior to the Son. In Irenaeus's image, the Son and the Spirit are the two hands of the Father. The Son was dependent upon the Spirit, and the Spirit was dependent upon the Son; in the New Testament, we see a deep reciprocity between them. Christ is, first, born of the Spirit; then anointed by the Spirit; then empowered by the Spirit to live a fully human life; and then, following his death and resurrection, exalted by the Spirit. As we have seen, the Spirit was Jesus' inseparable companion throughout his human life—from conception, baptism, wilderness temptations, the working of miracles and signs, to death and resurrection. The Spirit empowered, sustained, and renewed Jesus' life as a human being. The Spirit enabled him to live within the limits of human nature, to resist every temptation, and to follow the way of love and the path of suffering. From the Gospel narratives portraying Jesus' life with the Spirit, we can conclude that "[t]he Son is Son, not solely because he shares the divine nature, but because he is in constant interaction with the Father receiving and giving the Spirit."[18]

The Western Christian tradition, as we saw in Chapter Two, has tended to subordinate, depersonalize, and marginalize the role of the Spirit. To redress this strong tendency, we need to state clearly that *the work of the Spirit is just as important as the work of the Son*. That might be a jolting statement to some. Christian faith is centered in Christ, of course, but Christ is not the whole story. Scripture bears witness to two sendings: the sending of the Spirit and the sending of the Son. The mission of Christ is set alongside the mission of the Spirit (Gal. 4:4–5). And these missions are intertwined and equal.

The Spirit was sent from the Father through the Son; the ministry of the Spirit is to lead us through the Son to the Father. What the Spirit was to Jesus as the incarnate Son, the Spirit becomes to us as the Father's adopted children.

So while insisting—against the thrust of the Western Christian tradition—that the role and status of the Spirit is just as important as that of the Son, we must also point to what we might call the self-effacing role of the Spirit in the Trinity. We could say that the Spirit is, in the arresting phrase of Yves Congar, "the person without a face."[19] This metaphor is not meant to diminish the distinct personhood and equality of the Spirit but simply to underscore how the Spirit works to magnify the Son as the way to the Father. As Jesus said of the Spirit, "he will not speak on his own authority, but whatever he hears he will speak, . . . He will glorify me" (John 16:13–14). We could paraphrase it this way: "the Spirit draws attention to the Son." In the language of John's Gospel, the Spirit's work is glorifying the Son and the Father. The act of glorifying, we could say, is an act of witnessing. In Scripture the Spirit seems always to be saying, "Look not at me, but at the Father and his Son." James Packer uses the image of a floodlight to capture this role: a well-placed floodlight bathes a building or other object in light, but we are not supposed to focus attention on where the light comes from. So the Spirit is "the hidden floodlight shining on the Savior."[20]

Clearly in the New Testament a primary work of the Spirit is to initiate us into two primary relationships that are focused on two confessions: "Jesus is Lord," and "*Abba*, Father." Paul stated, "No one can say, 'Jesus is Lord,' except by the Holy Spirit" (1 Cor. 12:3), and "Because you are sons, God sent the Spirit of his Son into our hearts, the Spirit who calls out, '*Abba*, Father'" (Gal. 4:6). The Spirit's focus is not to shine the light on the Spirit's self but to open up our lives to the Son and the Father, witnessing to, manifesting, and glorifying. We can say that the "mission of the Spirit is to glorify the Son and we are most honoring of the Spirit when our attention is most focused on Christ."[21]

In the creed, the Spirit is called "Lord and giver of life." The Spirit gives life but is not the source of it (that is the Father), and is not the model or prototype of it (that is the incarnate Son). The Spirit brings that life to us so that we actually experience it. If some of the images of the Spirit in the New Testament—wind, fire, and water—are impersonal images, they are for the purpose of conveying deep dimensions of personal being and relationship, pointing to the way the Spirit of God works deep within us and in the body of Christ. The Spirit's working is like the wind, blowing where it wills, like fire uncontained and consuming, like water flowing, refreshing and life-giving.

The Trinity and Life in the Spirit

The classic doctrine of the Trinity grew out of the deep threefold pattern of relationality between the Father, the Son, and the Spirit that we see throughout the New Testament. Though a rich mystery, the Trinity is a crucially practical doctrine—practical in the sense that it fundamentally shapes our practices as Christian communities. For the way we understand God's manner of loving and relating sets the model for how God's followers conduct their lives together and carry out their mission in the world. And we need a practical understanding of the Trinity in which to frame a fuller doctrine of the Spirit. As Lesslie Newbigin observed, "Recovery of a practical faith in the power of the Holy Spirit will lead us astray if it is not held firmly with an equally practical Trinitarian faith."[22]

So finally, I examine some of the ways the doctrine of the Trinity functions to focus and sustain the Christian life, and to keep in check the distortions and imbalances to which that life is prone.[23] Put in Trinitarian terms, we can say that Christian discipleship means following the risen Christ, in the power of the Holy Spirit, to the glory and praise of the God the Father. Each of these three truths provides a check against serious and common distortions of the Christian way.

Following the Risen Christ

The Christian life, whatever else it may be, is a life of obedience and discipleship to Jesus Christ. It includes bringing good news to the poor, releasing captives, healing and caring for the sick, delivering the oppressed, all of which is part of participating in the kingdom of God that Jesus inaugurated. It means taking up the cross and following Jesus, walking in his way of loving and serving, his way of treating enemies, his way of giving and forgiving. It means, in short, imitating Jesus. It involves training in self-renunciation, counting the cost, renouncing lordship over people, and gaining a new attitude toward money and possessions. It is a visible and very concrete path of obedience and sacrifice. It takes on a kingdom-building, cruciform shape.

This focus of life in the Spirit is a check against triumphalism, spiritual elitism, authoritarianism, and experientialism. Triumphalism claims that resurrection life has superseded life under the cross, that the Christian life is a life of uninterrupted bounty, success, and triumph. Its close cousin, spiritual elitism, claims that possessing certain spiritual gifts and powers places one on a higher spiritual plain, well above the ordinary believer. Standing against both is the call to cruciform discipleship, to follow Jesus in the way of self-giving love.

Authoritarianism is the fleshly desire to control, manipulate, and lord over people, variously exercised under the claims of "divine anointing," kingdom efficiency, and scriptural precedent. The way of Jesus always says "no" to these types of behaviors. Rather than seeking greatness, Jesus washes his disciples' feet with a basin and towel (John 13:5). Spiritual experientialism is the hankering after miraculous visitations and running after supernatural sensations, the seeking of one spiritual thrill after another. To this, Jesus says things like, "Come, follow me. Love your neighbor as yourself. Feed my sheep. Deliver the oppressed. Heal and care for the sick. Proclaim good news to the poor. "As much as you for one of the least of these, you did it unto me" (Mark 1:17, 12:31; Lk. 4:18–21; John 21:17; Matt. 25:40). The call to following Jesus is always a call to obedience, to faithful burden-bearing, to patient endurance, to forgiveness, and to tangible acts of love.

In the Power of the Spirit

The Christian life, whatever else it may be, is a life indwelt and empowered by the Spirit of God. For Paul the term "spiritual" refers specifically to the life produced by the presence and work of the Holy Spirit. The Spirit is basically God's presence in power/weakness among God's people. The Spirit dwells in Christians, indeed can fill us, and the location of that indwelling is the "heart" (2 Cor. 1:22; 3:3; Gal. 4:6; Rom. 2:29; 5:6). The Spirit is the source of transformation and Christlikeness in disciples, the very life of God coursing in us and through us.

This focus of the Christian life is a check against moralism, legalism, rationalism, and Bible deism. When the work of the Spirit is diminished, discipleship, with its stress on obedience, sacrifice, and righteousness, quickly becomes moralistic and legalistic. Moralism is the confidence that we can get better and better if we just try harder and harder. And legalism—a natural and constant human propensity—reduces relationship to rule-keeping. The Spirit counters all moralism and legalism by inviting us into the intimacy and joy—the ecstasy—of God's life, indeed, by being the bearer of that life.

Rationalism treats God more as an idea or rational principle than a person, thus diminishing or even denying true relationality. And Bible deism, which is a form of rationalism, confines our relationship with God to ingesting the words of the Bible. Against both, the focus on the power and presence of the Spirit upholds the personal, experiential, and intimate character of life with God.

To the Glory and Praise of God the Father

The Christian life, whatever else it may be, is a life devoted to the glory of God the Father and the coming of God's kingdom. At the heart of the biblical story is the almighty Creator God, maker of heaven and earth, the one who sustains the world and human life in it. God is personally and passionately involved in the created order but totally distinct from it, never to be identified with the forces of nature. The Father is the elusive transcendent one who will not be domesticated or brought under human control. The created order is a theater of the divine glory, and human life finds its proper end in the praise of God.

This focus of the Christian life is a check against all idolatries, magic, and domestication of the faith. Idolatry is a constant human temptation, for we are creatures prone, at every moment, to fashion God in our own image. Scripture makes it clear that idolatry, at its core, is a religious disguise for self-centeredness. Idols are projections of the human will. They represent attempts to make God less transcendent, less elusive, less sovereign and free, more at the beck and call of human interests.

The practice of magic is a close corollary. Magic is the attempt to manipulate God or the "gods" through the use of "automatic" techniques like incantations, spells, sacred objects, and the like. It is blatant and frightening when it appears in black magic and the occult, but it takes much more subtle form when Christian practices and beliefs get recast as "automatic" techniques to summon or control God.

Focus on God the Father resists the powerful and deep human impulses to bind God to human agendas through idolatry and magic. It enables us to critique and resist the domestication of God in the service of personal, economic, and social interests.

~

Christian life is Trinitarian. It means following the risen Christ, in the power of the Spirit, to the glory of the Father and the coming of God's kingdom. Spiritual life focused mainly on the Father or on the Son or on the Spirit will become imbalanced and problematic. A balanced spirituality will be marked by (1) a strong sense of the goodness of the Father's creation, and corresponding engagement with the world; (2) emphasis on reconciliation with God through the Son, and the preaching of the gospel of the kingdom; and (3) an openness to the Spirit's presence and power, and a reliance on that power as the church engages in God's mission.

NOTES

[1] Gordon Fee, *Paul, the Spirit, and the People of God* (Peabody, MA: Hendrickson, 1996), 38.

[2] Robert Jenson, *The Triune Identity: God According to the Gospel* (Philadelphia: Fortress, 1982), 44.

[3] Eugene Rogers, *After the Spirit: A Constructive Pneumatology from Resources outside the Modern West* (Grand Rapids: Eerdmans, 2005), 76.

[4] John Meier, *Matthew* (Wilmington, DE: Michael Glazier, 1980), 372.

[5] Francis Watson, "Trinity and Community: A Reading of John 17," *International Journal of Systematic Theology* 1 (1999): 170.

[6] Watson, "Trinity and Community," 169.

[7] Wesley Hill, *Paul and the Trinity: Persons, Relations, and the Pauline Letters* (Grand Rapids: Eerdmans, 2015), and Matthew Bates, *The Birth of the Trinity: Jesus, God, and Spirit in New Testament and Early Christian Interpretations of the Old Testament* (New York: Oxford, 2015). Hill argues that many modern New Testament scholars have been essentially "binitarian," assuming that Paul is best interpreted "by keeping the Spirit's identity and action in a secondary, derivative place from those of God and Jesus. But that . . . is a perspective exegesis will not support" (165).

[8] Lesslie Newbigin, *Trinitarian Doctrine for Today's Mission* (1963; Eugene, OR: Wipf & Stock, 2006), 34.

[9] For a moving glimpse into this process in the lives of early Christians, see Robert L. Wilkins, *The Spirit of Early Christian Thought: Seeking the Face of God* (New Haven: Yale University, 2005), especially 85–109.

[10] Irenaeus, *Against Heresies* 4.38.3

[11] Gregory of Nyssa, in *Christology of the Later Fathers*, ed. E. R. Hardy and C. C. Richardson, Library of Christian Classics (Philadelphia: Westminster John Knox, 1954), 262.

[12] In general, see James D. G. Dunn, "Spirit, Holy Spirit," *New Bible Dictionary* (Downers Grove, IL: InterVarsity, 1996), 1125–27.

[13] Raymond Brown, "The Paraclete in the Fourth Gospel," *New Testament Studies* 13, no. 2 (1966–67): 113–32.

[14] Rogers, *After the Spirit*, 46.

[15] Gregory of Nazianzus, *Fifth Theological Oration*, in *Nicene and Post-Nicene Fathers* 2, 7, p. 327.

[16] In 1 Peter 4:14, the same word is applied to Christians: "If you are insulted because of the name of Christ, you are blessed, for the Spirit of Glory and of God rests upon you." Numerous other Greek verbs were used in LXX to convey the presence of the Spirit upon its object: come upon, be upon, descends, hover, falls upon, overshadows, dwells in. (e.g., Lk. 1:35; 2:25; Matt 3:16; Acts 10:44; Lk. 9:34; Rom 8:9, 11).

[17] Jürgen Moltmann, *The Way of Jesus Christ: Christology in Messianic Dimensions*, translated by Margaret Kohl (1989, Minneapolis, MN: Fortress Press, 1993), 150. See the Nicene Creed with this addition at the back of this book.

[18] Thomas Smail, *The Giving Gift: The Holy Spirit in Person* (London: Hodder, 1988), 97.

[19] Yves Congar, *I Believe in the Holy Spirit* (London: Geoffrey Chapman, 1983), 3:5.

[20] James Packer, *Keep in Step with the Spirit* (Downers Grove, IL: InterVarsity, 1984), 66.

[21] Smail, *Giving Gift*, 31.

[22] Lesslie Newbigin, *Trinitarian Doctrine for Today's Mission*, 83.

[23] This section is adapted from my book *Participating in God's Life* (Abilene, TX: Leafwood Publishers, 2003), 172–75, co-authored with Danny Swick.

KINGDOM

The Spirit is the power of God's reign that, beginning with the anointing of Jesus and then the event of Pentecost, is breaking into the old order of brokenness and death.

Every coming of the Spirit is an eschatological act, because in it the ultimate future to which God is leading us invades, touches, and transforms our temporal lives.
—Thomas Smail

The Spirit is given to make God's future real in the present. That is the first, and perhaps most important, point to grasp about the work of this strange personal power.
—N. T. Wright

In the New Testament, the Spirit of God and the kingdom of God are closely related. The key connection is this: the Spirit is the power of God's inbreaking reign or kingdom. In Paul, the Spirit is the "first installment" or "down payment" of the kingdom (2 Cor. 1:21–22). In the Synoptic Gospels, the kingdom is present in Jesus because the Spirit is upon him and has anointed him to preach the good news of the kingdom (Lk. 4:18). When Jesus said, "The kingdom of God is among you" (Lk. 17:21), Luke underscores that the reign of God was being realized in and through Jesus because he possessed the Spirit.

For both Paul and the Gospel writers, the "last things" have begun occurring in history through the presence and power of the Spirit. Through the Spirit, the end of time begins to appear in the middle of time. The future is arriving in the present. This chapter shows the basic ways that the New Testament portrays this most essential aspect of the Spirit's role.

The New Exodus

In the Jewish heritage, the Spirit was to be a key part of God's end-time restoration envisioned by the prophets. The prophets envisioned a Spirit-filled "age to come," a new and powerful dawning of God's reign or kingdom, a breaking into the present of the age of the Messiah.

Jeremiah and Ezekiel's visions of the Messiah and the new covenant (Jer. 31:31–34; Ezek. 37) formed a basis for Jewish expectations, as did Isaiah's vision for a New Exodus (Isa. 40–55). The anointing of the Spirit, first on the Son of God at his Jordan River experience and then at Pentecost as a mighty wind and fire, was the sign that the messianic age—the age to come—had arrived.

Jesus was anointed by the Spirit at his baptism in the Jordan (Lk. 3:21–22). Luke demonstrates the significance of this Spirit anointing by clearly marking a path from the banks of the Jordan right to the entrance of the Nazareth synagogue: first, Jesus was "led by the Spirit" into forty days of wilderness temptation (4:1), and then "in the power of the Spirit" returned to Galilee to teach in the synagogues (4:14–15). In the Nazareth synagogue, Jesus, reading from Isaiah (42:6–7; 61:1), proclaimed that the Spirit had anointed him to preach "good news to the poor," "release to the captives," recovery of "sight to the blind," "to set the oppressed free," and "proclaim the year of the Lord's favor" (Lk. 4:18–19).

Recent scholars interpret Jesus' anointing with the Spirit in light of Isaiah's New Exodus images.[1] In Isaiah 40–55, the prophet used Exodus typology to envision a New Exodus through which God's people would be delivered from exile and become a witness to the nations. The basic features of that vision include the following:

1. A way will be opened up in the wilderness (Isa. 40:3–5).
2. The Lord will overcome Israel's oppressors and release them from oppression (42:13–15).

3. He will lead them in a glorious procession along a way through the wilderness, with his presence in front of them and behind them (52:11–12).
4. He will sustain them in the wilderness, providing rivers in the desert and abundant food (41:17–20; 43:19–21; 49:9–10).
5. God will pour the restoring Spirit upon them and their descendants (44:3–5) and teach and lead them in his way (54:13).
6. The goal of this New Exodus will be God's enthronement in a restored Zion (a New Jerusalem).
7. It will be accomplished by a servant-king who is also a prophet-liberator (like Moses).[2]

This New Exodus is "the fresh and final repetition of ancient Israel's greatest story."[3] For Luke, this imagery is a central way of speaking about the salvation that Jesus' ministry inaugurates.[4]

It begins with John the Baptist, who is the "voice of one crying in the wilderness, 'Prepare the way of the Lord'" (Lk. 3:4, quoting Isa. 40:3); it reaches a key moment in the baptismal anointing (Lk. 3:22), where the Spirit empowers Jesus as divine son, anointed Davidic king, and servant of the Lord (cf. Isa. 42:1 with Lk.. 3:22); it continues in the testing of Jesus' royal sonship in the wilderness (Lk. 4:1–13); and then comes to a focus in the messianic mission as defined in the Nazareth sermon (Lk. 4:18–21; cf. Isa. 61:1–2), an episode that for Luke appears to inaugurate the New Exodus.

As noted previously, in the Nazareth episode, the Spirit anoints Jesus for five tasks (preach good news to the poor, release the captives, give sight to the blind, free the oppressed, and proclaim the acceptable year of the Lord). The first four tasks all involve images of Israel's low and broken estate from Isaiah 40–55—they are poor, captive, blind, and oppressed. And all five tasks point to her impending release from this condition by the Spirit-anointed servant of the Lord and royal Son. The mission of Jesus, according to Luke, is to release Israel from her poverty, captivity, and blindness, and to bring her through the wilderness "way" to a New Zion.

Jesus' miracles of healing and exorcism, done through the power of the Spirit upon him, would then be seen as the expected New Exodus miracles—specific fulfillments of Isaiah 61:1–2. That is exactly what we find in Luke 7 when John's disciples ask Jesus, "Are you he who is to come, or should we expect someone else?" "Go back and report to John," Jesus replies, "what you have seen and heard: the blind receive sight, the lame walk, those who have leprosy are cleansed, the deaf hear, the dead are raised up, and the good news is proclaimed to the poor" (Lk. 7:20–22). Luke clearly views the Spirit as the source of these liberating deeds, as we see in Peter's short speech in Acts 10. Peter tells "how God anointed Jesus of Nazareth with the Holy Spirit and power; how he went about doing good and healing all who were oppressed by the devil, because God was with him" (Acts 10:38). The passage appears to be closely connected to the Nazareth sermon in Luke 4, and serves as an extension and illustration of it.[5] The Spirit clearly is the power in Jesus' ministry; indeed, the kingdom is present where the Spirit is at work through Jesus.

In the Gospels, a clear picture emerges: "Jesus, the anointed one, inspired by the Spirit, was the end-time prophet who broke the long drought of the Spirit and introduced the new age of the Spirit in himself and his mission."[6]

Throughout Jesus' earthly ministry, we can say that the Spirit was the dominant partner. Jesus was conceived by the Spirit, anointed by the Spirit, led by the Spirit (Lk. 4:1), strengthened by the Spirit in temptation and trial, empowered by the Spirit to work miracles and exorcisms, and sustained by the Spirit through his passion and death. But a key transition occurs with Jesus' resurrection and ascension.

As Acts opens, the resurrected Christ has appeared to the disciples over a forty-day period and taught them about "the kingdom of God." They ask him, "Lord, are you at this time going to restore the kingdom to Israel?" Jesus' answer (Acts 1:8), using three allusions to Isaiah, points once again to the hope for Israel's restoration. First, he says, "You will receive power when the Holy Spirit comes upon you"—an allusion to Isaiah 32:15 and the New Exodus transformation of Israel's wilderness state. Second, he says, "You will be my witnesses"—an allusion to Isaiah 43:10–12, where restored Israel is given this very commission. And third, he says that they will be his witnesses "to the ends of the earth"—which takes up the last line of Isaiah

49:6: "I will also make you a light for the Gentiles that my salvation may reach to the ends of the earth." (Paul claims this same verse as his commission from the risen Lord [Acts 13:47].)

In his account of the Pentecostal outpouring in Acts 2, Luke quotes the prophet Joel to indicate the long-awaited "last days"—the promised age to come—are upon them, where God is pouring out his Spirit "on all people." This is happening because God raised Jesus from the grave and exalted him. God has made him both Lord and Christ. Luke combines the theme of Jesus as the long-awaited Davidic king and Messiah with the theme of the prophet-like Moses. Jesus has been exalted to the eternal throne of David, a throne not in Jerusalem but at God's right hand (Acts 2:33–35; Ps. 110:1). He is also portrayed as a greater Moses who ascends to God in order to receive a new gift for Israel—not the gift of the law brought down from Mount Sinai, but the gift of the Spirit, the covenant renewer, poured out on Pentecost (Acts 3:22–23).[7]

Jesus' resurrection and ascension thus mark a decisive change in his relationship with the Spirit. No longer dependent upon the Spirit as during his ministry on earth, now as the exalted one he receives the Spirit in a new way; he receives from the Father the promised Spirit, becoming Lord of the Spirit. Jesus transitions from being the Spirit-bearer, the promised one who was filled with the Spirit, to the Spirit-sender. Now he becomes the one who gives the Spirit, fulfilling God's prophecy through Joel that "I will pour out my Spirit on all people" (Acts 2:33; Joel 2:28). The Spirit of God now becomes also the "Spirit of Jesus" (Acts 16:7). "The Spirit now is not simply a mysterious power, but a power stamped with the character of Jesus."[8] Now, we might say, the Spirit has become the executive power of the ascended Messiah, enabling Jesus to continue from his exalted place what he began in his ministry on earth. Christ is no absentee Messiah.

Through the gift of the Spirit, the Messiah has brought a new cleansing, restoration, and transformation of Israel and set in motion the witness to the "ends of the earth." The promise of a New Exodus is being fulfilled. John the Baptist's promise that the Messiah would cleanse with Spirit and fire (Lk. 3:16) is fulfilled. God's end-time rule has broken in and been focused uniquely through Jesus Christ, the unique man of the Spirit.

So Peter on Pentecost connects the breaking in of the "last days" to Jesus of Nazareth, the anointed one. He tells the story of Jesus' life, death, resurrection, and exaltation (Acts 2:22–36). And when the multitude asks what they should do, Peter tells them: "Repent and be baptized, every one of you, in the name of Jesus Christ for the forgiveness of your sins. And you will receive the gift of the Holy Spirit" (2:38). Three thousand people are baptized. Baptism marks their initiation into the end-time community of the Messiah, the sphere of the Spirit where they begin to experience the resurrection life of God's kingdom and are equipped with the Spirit to continue the mission of (new) Israel to the nations.

The New Temple

In addition to the promise of a New Exodus, the Spirit-filled "age to come" envisioned by Israel's prophets included the vision of a new, end-time temple and the return of God's presence in the midst of God's people. Here too the Spirit was to be a key to God's end-time restoration.

Here is how the law and the prophets put it:

> In the last days
> > the mountain of the LORD's temple will be established
> > > as the highest of the mountains;
> > it will be exalted above the hills,
> > > and all nations will stream to it.
> Many peoples will come and say,
> > "Come, let us go up to the mountain of the LORD,
> > > to the temple of the God of Jacob.
> > He will teach us his ways,
> > > so that we may walk in his paths." (Isaiah 2:2–3; Micah 4:1–3)

> I will put my dwelling place among you, and I will not abhor you. I will walk among you and be your God, and you will be my people. (Lev. 26:11–12)

> I will make a covenant of peace with them; it will be an everlasting covenant. I will establish them and increase their numbers, and I will put

> my sanctuary among them forever. My dwelling place will be with them;
> I will be their God, and they will be my people. (Ezek. 37:26-27)

The backstory to this vision of God's restored dwelling place or sanctuary is the story of God's presence with Israel through tabernacle and temple.

After the Lord delivers Israel from bondage in Egypt, Moses leads them through the desert to Mount Sinai, the place where God "dwells." On the mountain, Moses receives the Ten Commandments and then precise instructions for building a tabernacle (Exod. 25–31). The Lord plans to "move" from the mountain and dwell among the covenanted people by means of this tent (25:8; 29:42–3). When the tabernacle is complete, the guiding cloud came to rest upon it and "the glory of LORD filled the tabernacle" (40:35). The tabernacle became a space filled up with God, a place of the divine presence. God's presence was not confined to the tabernacle, but there was an intensity of presence not true of any other place.

With the sanctuary of presence in their midst, Israel set off to the land of promise and the place that "the LORD your God will choose as a dwelling for his name" (Deut. 12:11). That new dwelling, completed many years later, was Solomon's temple. When it was completed, "the glory of the LORD filled his temple" (1 Kings 8:11). But Israel's rebellion led eventually to the departure of the Lord's presence from the temple. In exile in Babylon, the prophet Ezekiel saw a vision of the departure of the Lord's glory from the Jerusalem temple (Ezek. 11:22–23). But Ezekiel also envisioned a time of the Lord's dramatic return: "the glory of the Lord entered the temple through the gate facing east. Then, the Spirit lifted me up and brought me into the inner court; and the glory of the LORD filled the temple" (Ezek. 43:4–5). The vision is of an end-time temple to which God's presence will return.

In the Bible's rich temple-theology, both the tabernacle and the temple are miniature working models, we might say, of creation as God intended. They served as signs of God's intention to renew all of creation. In the coming age, God would begin the construction of an end-time temple, and the sanctuary of God would expand to fill the whole new heavens and new earth (Rev. 21–22).[9]

In Jesus, this end-time temple has been inaugurated. Following Jesus' cleansing of the temple, when the Jews asked him for a sign to support his actions, he answered, "Destroy this temple, and I will raise it again in three days." The Jews did not understand, since it had taken forty-six years to build Herod's temple; John clarifies that Jesus was speaking about the temple of his body (John 2:19–22). This reference to Jesus as a temple expands on John 1:14: "And the Word became flesh and tabernacled [pitched his tent] among us, and we beheld his glory." The word "tabernacled" is related to the Hebrew word *shekinah*, which refers to the glorious divine presence. God's glory that was formerly present in the Holy of Holies has now, in Jesus, burst into the world. In Jesus—the one anointed by the Spirit—the place of God's presence shifts from the temple in Jerusalem to the person of Jesus. As Mark's Gospel puts it, Jesus replaces "this temple made with human hands" with the temple of his resurrected body—a temple "not made with hands" (Mark 14:58).

So Jesus, in his encounter with the Samaritan woman, tells her that the time is coming when true worship will not be in the temple building but offered to God "in the Spirit and in truth" (John 4:21–26). He offers her "living water," saying that "whoever drinks the water I give them will never thirst"; indeed, it "will become in them a spring of water gushing up to eternal life" (4:13). This appears to be an allusion to Ezekiel's vision of the end-time temple, where a river of water is flowing out from underneath it; fish are abundant in its waters and fruit trees are flourishing along its banks (47:1–12).

This connection to the temple becomes stronger when Jesus is teaching in the temple on the last day of the feast of tabernacles:

> If anyone thirsts, let him come to me and drink. Whoever believes in me, as the Scripture has said, "Out of his heart will flow rivers of living water." Now this he said about the Spirit, whom those who believed in him were to receive, for as yet the Spirit had not been given, because Jesus was not yet glorified. (John 7:37–39 ESV)

In Ezekiel's vision, the waters flowed from the innermost part of the temple, the Holy of Holies, the place of God's presence. Now Jesus has become that temple, that presence. It is out of his "heart" that "flow rivers of living water." And that living water is the Spirit whom Jesus will pour out on his disciples at Pentecost.

The Lord had promised, "I will be their God, and they will be my people" (Ezek. 37:27). This promise was fulfilled through the Spirit in God's new end-time temple, first through the temple of Jesus' own body, crucified and resurrected, and then in Christ's body, the church.

Paul draws explicitly on the Old Testament imagery of God dwelling among the covenant people by means of tabernacle and temple. With Jesus Christ as the "chief cornerstone," the church "rises to become a holy temple in the Lord," and in it Christians are being "built together to become a dwelling in which God lives by his Spirit" (Eph. 2:21–22). "Don't you know that you yourselves are God's temple," Paul asks, "and that God's Spirit dwells in your midst? . . . . God's temple is sacred, and you together are that temple" (1 Cor. 3:16–17; also 6:19; 2 Cor. 6:16). Through the Spirit, the body of Christ, the church, continues the fulfillment of the end-time or eschatological temple proclaimed by the prophets.

The Spirit is none other than the way the presence of the Lord has returned to the midst of his people. As God's presence "filled" Moses' tabernacle and "filled" Solomon's temple, so the community of believers is "filled" with the Spirit and experiences the "fullness" of God (Eph. 5:18; 3:19). So when a pagan comes into the Christian assembly and his heart is laid open as the Spirit moves in the prophetic gift, according to Paul, he will "worship God and declare that God is really among you" (1 Cor. 14:24–25).

Christians live in the "dispensation of the Spirit" and thus can behold greater splendor than Moses did. Moses veiled his face from the Lord's presence when he came down the mountain. The temple also had a veil, shielding people from God's presence. But the Spirit of the Lord has removed the veil. Christians can enter the holy place and stand in the very presence of God. With unveiled faces, they can behold the glory of the Lord and in that presence be changed from one degree of glory to another (2 Cor. 3:12–18).

The final scene in Revelation pictures the emergence of the ultimate temple of God, which will be Eden restored in a new heavens and new earth. John saw "the Holy City, the new Jerusalem, coming down out of heaven from God, prepared as a bride beautifully dressed for her husband." A loud voice said, "Look! God's dwelling place is now among the people, and he will dwell with them. They will be his people, and God himself will be with them" (Rev. 21:2–3).

The New Exodus and the New Temple are both signs and means of the inauguration of God's new creation—to which we now turn.

The New Creation

Paul's core belief is that in Jesus the Messiah the "age to come" has burst into this "present age." Through the Spirit, the "last things" begin occurring in history. Christ is the first fruits of the resurrection-renewal of the age to come. Those "in Christ" will participate in the coming final harvest, but not only that: Through the Spirit of Christ we already share in the first fruits (Rom. 8:23). Through the Spirit we partake of the life to come.

This eschatological tension is embedded in the deep structure of New Testament thought. The Spirit poured out at Pentecost is the Spirit of God's future. Through the Spirit we experience the "powers of the coming age" (Heb. 6:5). In the Spirit, the powers of the age to come are let loose in the present age (Heb. 2:4; 1 Cor. 12:12; Acts 3:1–10; 5:12).

God's new creation has broken into the present age. The fulfillment of God's promise to Abraham has opened up a new era in God's redemptive plan. Through Jesus Christ, God has acted decisively to remake the world. The "new creation"—a new era—has broken into the present "evil" age, which "in its present form is passing away" (1 Cor. 7:31). Through faith in Christ and baptism into his death, believers have died to their old life and now participate in this new creation, where we "eagerly await by faith the righteousness for which we hope" (Gal. 5:5).

For Paul, "new creation" serves as "a shorthand signifier for the dialectical eschatology that runs throughout the New Testament."[10] The new creation already appears, but there is a strong "eschatological reservation," a "not yet" that will not allow us to assert the unqualified presence of God's kingdom. The powers of the old eon are doomed, already writhing in their death throes; the new creation is already appearing. But the full time is not yet. This basic eschatological tension runs throughout the New Testament, and provides the framework for perspective on discipleship in the present overlap of the ages. The community of faith is made up of those "on whom the culmination of the ages has come" (1 Cor. 10:11).

Paul understood the pouring out of the Spirit to be a key end-time event. This was shaped by four main themes in Old Testament prophecy about the Spirit in the end times—themes that the New Testament interprets as now fulfilled.

1. *The pouring out of the Spirit on the descendants of Israel* (Isa. 44:3; Joel 2:28–29). Pentecost represents a dramatic turning point between the old age and the new. In the old age, the Spirit visited Israel on certain occasions and in certain individuals, but in the new age, God pours out the Spirit, not just on kings and prophets, but on every believer as a permanent possession. Paul in 1 Corinthians 12:13 says that all believers "drink of one Spirit," a verse that alludes to Old Testament prophecies about the Spirit being poured out in the age that is to come.

2. *The gift of the Spirit within God's people* (Ezek. 37). Through Ezekiel the Lord declares, "I will put my Spirit in you, and you will live . . . . [you] shall follow my laws and be careful to keep my decrees. . . . My dwelling place will be with them" (Ezek. 37:14, 24, 27). This passage probably lies behind Paul's view that the Spirit dwells in believers and that they are temples of God's Spirit (Rom. 8:9; 1 Cor. 3:16).

3. *The Spirit and the new covenant* (Jer. 31). Through Jeremiah, the Lord says, "I will put my Law in their minds, and I will write it on their hearts. I will be their God, and they will be my people" (Jer. 31:33). Paul picks up this theme, emphasizing that the Law (old covenant) has been replaced by a new "law of the Spirit" (Rom. 8:1–4). Christians are ministers of a new covenant not of the letter but of the Spirit (2 Cor. 3:6; Rom. 7:6).

4. *The Messiah as bearer of the Spirit.* The promised Messiah would be endowed with the Spirit and his Spirit-empowered ministry would be marked by justice, gentleness, faithfulness, wisdom, power, and fear of God (Isa. 11:2–3; 42:1–4).

In the New Testament, we see an intricate connection between the Spirit of God and the coming reign of God. Christians live in two times (or ages or eons) simultaneously. The difference between them is not that one age simply follows another—the current or old age followed by the age to come. Rather the "age to come" has broken into the "old age." The old age is characterized by rebellion against God, violence, exploitation, sin, and death. But the new age has broken into the old through the triumph of Christ in his cross and resurrection, and he has ascended to the right hand of his Father where he is presently reigning.

Throughout the New Testament, the whole of Christian life is framed by this eschatological tension. All things have become new (2 Cor. 5:17). Redemption is both already and not yet (Eph. 1:7; 4:30); our adoption as God's children is already and not yet (Rom. 8:15, 23).

For Paul there are two resurrections—Christ's was the first fruits, and the Christian's will surely follow. We live between the times of the two resurrections, having already been "raised with Christ" in our baptism and awaiting our future bodily resurrection (Rom. 8:10–11).

In some passages, Paul's stress is on the inbreaking of the new creation in the present—the "already." A new world is bursting upon the scene (2 Cor. 5:17). This focus on the "already" serves to call believers away from the traditional ways of the old age and to take hold of the new that has broken in.

In other passages, Paul's focus is on the "not yet" character of the new creation. Though a new world is bursting upon the scene, it remains situated in the midst of the old. There is still much groaning for the fullness of the new, much waiting in eager longing for the "revealing of the children of God."

Three important metaphors capture the basic eschatological tension in Paul's understanding of the Spirit.[11]

Firstfruits (Rom. 8:23; cf. 14–30). This is one of the clearest texts setting out Paul's eschatological framework. As the "firstfruits," the Spirit provides both evidence and guarantee—evidence of our adoption as God's children and status as joint heirs with Christ, and guarantee of our final adoption, which is the redemption of our bodies. "But we ourselves, who have the firstfruits of the Spirit, groan inwardly as we wait eagerly for our adoption to sonship, the redemption of our bodies" (8:23).

What believers experience now of the Spirit as firstfruits is continuous with what they will experience at the full harvest. "The Spirit is not a mere pointer toward the *eschaton*, but is the actual firstfruits of it."[12] And note that Paul uses "firstfruits" to refer both to Christ and the Spirit, indicating the deep connection between Christ and the Spirit in God's final purpose. Christ is the firstfruits of the resurrection, the first human being to be raised (1 Cor. 15:20); and if he was raised, so shall we. And we will have the same kind of "spiritual body" he has (15:44–49). And like Christ, we will live in full harmony with the Spirit—complete transformation accomplished by the Spirit and conformed to the image of Christ.

Down payment or guarantee (2 Cor. 1:21–22; 5:5; Eph. 1:14). God has given us "his Spirit in our hearts as a first installment (*arrabon*)" (2 Cor. 1:22 NRSV). This is a term used only in reference to the Spirit in the New Testament. The New International Version translates it in both 2 Corinthians passages as "a deposit, guaranteeing what is to come." The Spirit is "the certain evidence that the future has come into the present, the sure guarantee that the future will be realized in full measure."[13]

Seal (2 Cor. 1:21–22; Eph. 1:13–14; 4:30). In all three texts, the seal is the Spirit, by whom God has marked and claimed Christians as his own. And the seal provides an eschatological guarantee: "you were sealed for the day of redemption" (Eph. 4:30). John Levison interprets Paul's use of "seal" and "pledge" (*arrabon*)—used together in both 2 Corinthians 1 and Ephesians 1—against the backdrop of the Old Testament story of Judah and Tamar (Gen. 38).[14] Both terms, "seal" and "pledge," figure prominently in the story. Tamar dresses up like a prostitute to deceive her father-in-law, Judah, to entice him to have sex with her and produce an heir. Judah has nothing to pay her, and so gives her three items in pledge, one of them his "seal." Why would Paul use this story? One answer is that one of the twins produced from the union was the ancestor of David—and of the Messiah. God's promises were fulfilled in this most unusual way. The filling of the Spirit sets one in this long arc—the God who fulfilled the promises to the ancestors will certainly fulfill the bold promises to Christians. As Paul says in this context, in Christ "all the promises of God find their Yes" (2 Cor. 1:20, ESV). The Spirit of God is just such a pledge and seal.

But the reality of the "not yet" means waiting and expecting (Gal. 3:2; 5:5, 16). The Spirit assists in our waiting. We are "to wait for his Son from heaven" (1 Thess. 1:10), "await by faith the righteousness for which we hope" (Gal. 5:5), "wait . . . patiently" (Rom. 8:25), and "wait eagerly for our adoption" (Rom. 8:23); indeed, "all creation waits with *eager longing*" (Rom. 8:19, ESV). "Eager longing" is a phrase unique among Christian writers. It means something like the English idioms "craning the neck in anticipation" and "standing on tiptoe."[15] Creation suffers in bondage to decay; but it longs to see God's finished work of re-creation (Rom. 8:20–21). The present experience of the Spirit is rich but not yet complete. We long for the new creation to be brought to perfection in the redemption of our bodies.

But waiting is not passive. It involves readiness. Jesus said, "You also must be ready, because the Son of Man will come at an hour when you do not expect him." (Lk. 12:40). We are to "make ready"—that is, do the work God has called us to do. We are to continue the mission that Jesus began. As with Jesus, this too is enabled by the Spirit.

Believers not only know by faith how history will end; they also presently participate in that end through the presence of God's Spirit. We are those, Paul said, "on whom the culmination of the ages has come" (1 Cor. 10:11). Knowing this truth and experiencing this power, the disciple can follow Jesus in all things, even in those things that don't make sense to normal life in this world.

The Newness Recedes

As we have seen, the Spirit is the power of God's future breaking into the present. But in the postbiblical period, the doctrine of the Spirit began to be gradually divorced from eschatology. From about the third century onward, in fact, they lose their relationship to one another. The Spirit becomes the dispenser of grace through the church and the inspirer of its Scriptures, not so much the compelling force of an end-time community. The robust eschatological vision of the New Testament recedes as the church becomes more institutionalized and powerful.

The growth of the church's institutional reach and power brought a new way of understanding New Testament eschatological texts. When everyone became a church member in the Christian empire, both the level of committed discipleship in the church and the level of expectation for the inbreaking of God's new order—the kingdom—diminished in tandem. The visible church became such a mixed company that the "true church" had to be designated an "invisible" community revealed only at the last judgment. And the Spirit, the power of that inbreaking kingdom, increasingly became the (tamed) possession of the institutional church.[16]

This shift in Western Christianity gave rise to two quite different views of eschatology. The dominant view became "increasingly dualistic: this life is a preparation for the next, a training ground for a future destiny. The other stresses more strongly the [Christian] community as the place where the conditions of the life to come may be realized in the here and now." The first view has generally characterized the "orthodox" mainstream of Western Christendom; the second has been embodied mainly by renewal groups often judged heretical by the established churches.[17]

At the heart of this divergence was the doctrine of the Holy Spirit. Colin Gunton and others have argued that the mainstream Western tradition, when measured against the New Testament, was marked by a major deficiency in its doctrine of the Spirit. The New Testament, as we have seen, emphasizes the eschatological dimensions of the Spirit: the way the Spirit makes real in the present life of the community the victory of Jesus over the powers and brings rich foretastes of God's new creation. But the Western church has tended to postpone the effects of Jesus' victory to the promise of heaven and "the Spirit has tended to be institutionalized, so that in place of the free, dynamic, personal and particular agency of the Spirit, he is made into a substance which becomes the possession of the church. . . . [The result is] *claiming* too much of a realization of eschatology, while *expecting* too little of the community as a whole."[18]

In other words, Christendom tended to demonstrate an over-realized eschatology (in the institution of the church) and an under-realized discipleship (in the lives and fellowship of its members). The Spirit's present end-time work in the church was minimized. Rather than an end-time community where salvation is presently being experienced, the church becomes an institution where people are (often moralistically) prepared for a future salvation. The church becomes a kind of holding tank, a place to wait for rescue and for heaven, rather than an end-time community, a colony of heaven, where the Spirit gifts every member for ministry and where the Spirit's presence brings rich tastes of the heavenly banquet.

The difference between these two conceptions of eschatology and the church lies most basically in the doctrine of the Spirit and how the Spirit constitutes the church. The New Testament emphasizes the present eschatological work of the Spirit—the inbreaking of God's future—and the Spirit's freedom and dynamism for ministry and mission in the community. Later Christian tradition, after the Constantinian settlement, tended to institutionalize the Spirit and assume that Christians were mostly only *preparing* for the end, not already *partaking* partially of it.

N. T. Wright captures the contrast: "To postpone the effectiveness of his [Jesus'] victory to an after-life, as has been done so often in the Christian tradition, or to transform it into the victory of true ideas over false ones . . . is to fail to take seriously his stark prayer for the kingdom to come, and God's will to be done, on earth as it is in heaven." The first Christians followed neither of these two options: "they announced and celebrated the victory of Jesus over evil, as something that had already happened, something that related pretty directly to the real world, their world. There was still a mopping-up battle to be fought, but the real victory had been accomplished. That was the basis of their announcement to the principalities and powers that their time was up. That was the basis of their remarkable joy."[19]

A weak or tamed doctrine of the Spirit, as in Christendom, correlates with a strictly futurist eschatology. A robust doctrine of the Spirit, as in the New Testament, supports an inaugurated eschatology.

The Spirit is the power of God's future breaking into the present, applying the victory of Jesus to the life and mission of the church. The Spirit is the principle or energy of movement. When the Spirit is separated from God's inbreaking kingdom—from a dynamic eschatology—the sense of a church on the move, on mission, gets diminished. The church gets settled and domesticated. "Without the principle of movement, the church is in danger of turning from a pilgrim people into a structure standing still. When this happens, glory is in stasis. In the splendor of its institutions, in the beauty of its liturgies, in the radiance of its saints, the earthly church is its own static end—in a word, triumphalism."[20]

This is why Gordon Fee can say that the feature of earliest Christianity that most distances us from it is the strong sense of being an eschatological community, the inbreaking kingdom of God, empowered and gifted for mission by the Spirit of God.

NOTES

[1] See, for example, Mark Strauss, *The Davidic Messiah in Luke-Acts: The Promise and Its Fulfillment in Lukan Christology* (Sheffield, UK: JSOT Press, 1995).

[2] R. E. Watts, "Consolation or Confrontation? Isaiah 40–55 and the Delay of the New Exodus," *Tyndale Bulletin* 41, no. 1 (1990): 31–59.

[3] N. T. Wright, "Imagining the Kingdom: Mission and Theology in Early Christianity," *NTWrightPage* (blog), October 26, 2011, http://ntwrightpage.com/2016/07/12/imagining-the-kingdom/.

[4] See J. Manek, "The New Exodus in the Books of Luke," *Novum Testamentum* 2, no. 1 (1958): 8–23. For the New Exodus theme in Paul, see N. T. Wright, *The Day the Revolution Began* (New York: HarperCollins, 2016), 263–94.

[5] Max Turner, *Power from on High: The Spirit in Israel's Restoration and Witness in Luke-Acts* (Sheffield, UK: Sheffield Academic Press, 1996), 261–64.

[6] James D. G. Dunn, *The Christ and the Spirit: Volume 2, Pneumatology* (Grand Rapids: Eerdmans, 1998), 335.

[7] Turner, *Power from on High*, 285–89.

[8] Dunn, *The Christ and the Spirit*, 341.

[9] On the Bible's complex and rich temple theology, see G. K. Beale, *The Temple and the Church's Mission: A Biblical Theology of the Dwelling Place of God* (Downers Grove, IL: InterVarsity, 2004).

[10] Richard Hays, *The Moral Vision of the New Testament: A Contemporary Introduction to New Testament Ethics* (New York: HarperCollins, 1996), 198.

[11] For what follows, see Gordon Fee, *God's Empowering Presence: The Holy Spirit in the Letters of Paul* (Peabody, MA: Hendrickson, 1994), 806–8.

[12] T. David Beck, *The Holy Spirit and the Renewal of All Things* (Eugene, OR: Wipf & Stock, 2007), 36.

[13] Fee, *God's Empowering Presence,* 807.

[14] John R. Levison, *Filled with the Spirit* (Grand Rapids: Eerdmans, 2009), 255–263.

[15] *Apokaradokia,* in Bauer, Danker, Arndt, and Gingrich, *A Greek-English Lexicon of the New Testament and Other Early Christian Literature*, 3rd edition (Chicago: University of Chicago, 2003), 112.

[16] John Yoder, *The Priestly Kingdom* (Notre Dame, IN: Notre Dame University, 1984), 136–37.

[17] Jürgen Moltmann commented, "After the West committed itself to the *filioque* in the Nicene Creed . . . and after the persecution of the so-called Enthusiasts by both the Protestant and the Catholic churches at the time of the Reformation, the experience and theology of the Spirit of God ceased to play much of a part in our churches." Jürgen Moltmann, *The Church in the Power of the Spirit*, trans. Margaret Kohl (Philadelphia: Fortress, 1977), xv.

[18] Colin Gunton, "The Community: The Trinity and the Being of the Church," *The Promise of Trinitarian Theology* (Edinburgh, Scotland: T & T Clark, 1991), 65.

[19] N. T. Wright, *Jesus and the Victory of God* (Minneapolis, MN: Fortress, 1996), 659.

[20] Kilian McDonnell, *The Other Hand of God: The Holy Spirit as the Universal Touch and Goal* (Collegeville, MN: Liturgical Press, 2003), 53.

MISSION

The Spirit is a missionary and calls, empowers, and guides disciples on God's mission to bring about the restoration of all things.

The point of the Spirit is to enable those who follow Jesus to take into all the world the news that he is Lord, that he has won the victory over the forces of evil, that a new world has opened up, and that we are to help make it happen.

—N. T. Wright

The church of Christ does not so much have a mission as the mission of Christ has a church.

—Adrian Hastings

God's mission in Scripture is the story of God's remaking of the world. The death and resurrection of Jesus is the crux, the pivot point. In this event, God's end-time age of righteousness and justice has erupted, unleashing "new creation." The Spirit of God is the sign, seal, and power of this emerging new creation.

God's mission is to make all things new, to offer people reconciliation (both to the self and to their enemies), and to fashion creation as a place for human flourishing (a place of *shalom*). Through the Spirit we are enabled to participate in this cosmic missional project.

Missio Dei

God's mission from near the beginning of the biblical story was to restore creation after human rebellion shattered its harmony and goodness. Human disobedience defiles creation, and the consequences spread throughout all nations and into every dimension of human life (Gen. 3–11). In response, God chooses one man, Abraham, and makes a covenant with him: God will bless him and his descendants and, through them, all the nations of earth (12:1–3). His descendants, the people of Israel, are to be a holy nation, "to keep the way of the Lord," to live out God's original design for human life, and thus to shine as a light to all the nations of the earth. "God's mission involves God's people living in God's way in the sight of the nations."[1]

When Abraham's descendants grow into a numerous people and find themselves enslaved in Egypt, the Lord hears their cries and remembers his covenant with Abraham. He liberates and redeems them, leading them out of Egypt, across the desert to Sinai, and there makes a covenant with them: "out of all nations you will be my treasured possession. Although the whole earth is mine, you will be for me a kingdom of priests and a holy nation" (Exod. 19:5–6). This will define the chosen role that Israel will play in the rest of the biblical story. They are to be God's alternative community, a kind of showcase to the world of the kind of life that God intends for all peoples—a "light to the nations" (Isa. 42:6). They will be the means the Lord uses to renew creation and all nations.

This covenant people is marked and identified by God's living presence in their midst. "Make a sanctuary for me," says the LORD, "and I will dwell among them" (Exod. 25:8). Following elaborate instructions, Israel builds a tabernacle in the desert, and when it is completed, the cloud of presence covers the tent and the Lord's glory fills it (40:34–38). God is among them to work in and through them to carry out the divine mission—to spread God's glory among the nations. It is God's interventions and presence in their midst that make the mission possible.

Israel settles in the land of Canaan, first as a tribal confederation ruled by judges then as a kingdom. They are placed there in the midst of pagan nations so that the people of God can shine as a light to them. As the prophet Ezekiel put it much later: "This is what the Sovereign LORD says:

This is Jerusalem, which I have set in the center of the nations, with countries all around her" (Ezek. 5:5). Jerusalem was meant to glow with the light of God's glory (Isa. 60:1–3). By allegiance to God's covenant, Israel was to put God's glory on display to the nations all around.

But Israel repeatedly failed to live out its calling. Judges records the frequent cycle of idolatry, divine judgment, crying out to the Lord, and God's deliverance. Instead of shining God's light to the nations, they themselves were overtaken by darkness. Under the monarchy that followed, the king was to play a decisive role in furthering God's mission through Israel. He was to resist and defeat the idolatrous nations around Israel and support the worship of God in the temple—the place of God's presence and symbol of the nation's duty to fill the earth with God's presence.

Prophets appear on the scene to challenge the king and the nation when they have broken God's covenant and forgotten their identity and mission. They critique the people's exploitation of the poor, their alliances with foreign powers, and their embrace of idolatry. They call Israel to worship Yahweh alone, and "to act justly and to love mercy" and to "let justice roll on like a river and righteousness like a never-failing stream" (Mic. 6:8; Amos 5:24). They call Israel back to God's mission to bless all the nations. And even if Israel fails to be that light to the nations, the prophets envision a time when God will fulfill the divine mission, regathering Israel through a Messiah, pouring out the Spirit on them, and using them to draw the nations to the one God.

Over many generations the prophets are unable to reverse the momentum of Israel's rebellion and idolatry. God's judgment ensues. The ten northern tribes are scattered by the Assyrians (722 BC), and the two southern tribes are exiled in Babylon (586 BC). The mission of God to bless the nations through the chosen people seems to have come to an end. But in the midst of this profound identity crisis, the prophets of the exile, Jeremiah and Ezekiel, envision new possibilities. They insist that God is still ruling over human history and that history is still moving toward the final establishment of God's kingship over all peoples. In God's time, like a shepherd, God will regather scattered Israel, purify them, and continue to use them to bless the nations.

What God did in the Exodus to deliver Israel from slavery in Egypt, God will do again in a New Exodus (Isa. 40–55). God will establish a new covenant with them (Jer. 31:31–34); God will give them a "new heart" (Jer. 17:9) and pour the restoring Spirit upon them, moving them to keep God's decrees (Isa. 44:3–5; Ezek. 34:25–31). The "last days" envisioned by the prophets would also bring a new end-time temple, a place of God's loving and powerful presence. "My dwelling place will be with them; I will be their God, and they will be my people" (Ezek. 37:27). This end-time temple will be a place out of which a life-giving river will flow, creating abundance all along its banks (Ezek. 47:1–12).

The new covenant, the new heart, the pouring out of the Spirit, the building of an expansive end-time temple of God's presence—all would be the means of renewing Israel's vocation to bless the nations. So Israel waits for the restoration of God's kingdom, the re-forming of a holy people with a mission to the nations.

Jesus comes declaring, "The time has come . . . The kingdom of God has come near. Repent and believe the good news!" (Mark 1:15). With Jesus' coming and his proclamation of God's reign in the power of the Spirit, the regathering of God's end-time people begins. This regathering was to take place in two stages: first, to gather and restore Israel, since God had first chosen them for his mission, and then, to draw the gentiles into God's covenant people. Israel must not only be regathered into a community but also renewed by the Spirit so they can carry out God's mission (see Ezek. 36:24–36; 37:15–28).

So Jesus focuses on the nation of Israel. The Gospels use the image of gathering sheep into the sheepfold; Jesus begins forming a little flock of the lost sheep of Israel to which he will give the kingdom (Matt. 10:6; Lk. 12:32). But the nations will be gathered as well: "I have other sheep that are not of this sheep pen. I must bring them also" (John 10:16). With this ingathering, the "last days" have begun.

The Spirit is the power at work in Jesus as he announces and demonstrates the presence of God's reign. His mission is directed against all forms of human and social brokenness; salvation involves God's healing and renewing of all dimensions of human life, even the nonhuman creation.

It involves encountering the demonic and idolatrous powers that oppress people, bring misery and enslavement, and distort the structures of society. Jesus' mission—God's mission—is to begin reversing the consequences of evil that have become embedded in the creation.

So the kingdom coming is a matter of power—power to overturn the reign of evil, to set free its victims, and to heal the brokenness in its wake. This power comes through the presence of God's Spirit upon Jesus. He has been anointed by the Spirit to heal, liberate, and announce the good news of the kingdom coming (Acts 10:38). God's power is being poured out to free the creation from sin, idolatry, brokenness, misery, and Satan, and to renew the *shalom* that God intended for human life—life characterized by human flourishing, justice, love, and gratitude.[2]

The community that forms around Jesus is marked by concern for justice or righteousness. As the prophets said of the coming Messiah, "I will put my Spirit on him, and he will bring justice to the nations" (Isa. 42:1). Justice involves setting things right that are estranged, broken, or oppressive. It is especially concerned for the weak and vulnerable in society. The Gospels, especially Luke, emphasize God's concern for the poor, the beggars, the lame, the sinners, and in general all those considered outcasts in society. They are all welcome at Jesus' table—a welcome that scandalizes those religious leaders devoted to the Jewish purity laws. Jesus welcomes three groups of people usually shunned by the "righteous": those with physical deformities (lepers, blind, lame), traitors to Israel (tax collectors), and political enemies (Samaritans and Romans).

Before the little group representing regathered Israel could be sent out to all the nations, Jesus' death on the cross and resurrection from the grave had to occur. For Luke, the cross of Jesus does two main things. First, it is the means by which the powers of darkness are defeated so that God's rule over creation can begin at last. Second, this victory is accomplished because the innocent Jesus dies the death of the guilty. At the cross it becomes clear that Jesus is taking upon himself the death that has been prophesied for the impenitent nation. He was the suffering servant of Isaiah 53, by whose stripes and wounds they will be healed. At the heart of the story of Jesus, we find not a wrathful God demanding blood and bent on killing his Son, but a covenant-keeping God who takes upon himself the full and deadly force of sin. The Son of God takes upon himself the weight of Israel's and the world's sins and dies under the accumulated force of evil. As a result, God's kingdom can now come in its fullness.

Jesus had launched the kingdom or rule of God. In his short public career, he had proclaimed the kingdom and demonstrated its presence through his teaching, healings, and exorcisms. God was re-establishing his rule over the broken and rebellious earth. Jesus' death was the climax. It was a victory over the powers of evil and darkness—achieved because Jesus "gave himself for our sins, to rescue us from the present evil age" (Gal. 1:4), thus freeing people from idolatry and enslavement to the powers they were worshipping. As N. T. Wright has often noted, in Scripture idolatry is the fundamental human problem; out of it flows sin, corruption of all sorts, and distortion of the divine image in humans. The death of Jesus was the decisive victory over the powers, setting people free to give themselves to the true worship of God and to join in God's mission to bring his kingdom "on earth as in heaven."[3]

If through his death Jesus won the decisive victory over the enslaving powers of evil, then through his resurrection from the dead and ascension to the right hand of the Father he becomes the exalted Lord. Jesus is exalted to the eternal throne of David; he receives all authority in heaven and on earth. It is the resurrected Christ who sends the disciples out on God's mission (Matt. 28:18–20; John 20:21–22). It is the resurrected and ascended Christ who receives the Spirit from his Father and who sends the Spirit to clothe them with "power from on high," empowering them for the end-time gathering of Israel and the nations (Lk. 24:48; Acts 2:33).

Missio Spiritus

The primary purpose of the pouring out of the Spirit upon the disciples was empowering them for mission. The mission of Jesus in the power of the Spirit would be passed on to his disciples: "You will receive power when the Holy Spirit comes on you," said the risen Jesus, "and you shall be my witnesses in Jerusalem, and in all Judea and Samaria, and to the ends of the earth" (Acts 1:8). After forty days of waiting in Jerusalem, the Spirit was "poured out" upon them on the day of Pentecost. Acts is a commentary on the Spirit's unrelenting focus on Jesus and empowering the proclamation of Jesus. "Acts is a book not about love but about power. Its fundamental theme is the triumphant march of the Spirit-empowered church throughout the Roman world."[4] It unfolds the story of how the witness spreads from Jerusalem following the pattern of Acts 1:8. At every point, the Spirit initiates and guides the mission. The following are some key features of the missional Spirit highlighted in Luke and Acts.

The Holy Spirit was poured out by the ascended Christ to continue the mission of Christ. Jesus' mission began with the anointing of the Spirit (Lk. 3:21–22), and the church's mission begins with the pouring out of the Spirit (Acts 2:11–13). Just as Jesus was empowered by the Spirit to proclaim good news to the poor and to bind up the brokenhearted (Lk. 4:18), so the Spirit empowers the church to continue that mission of proclaiming and healing (Acts 10:38; 2:17–18). The Spirit empowered Jesus for his mission, and the Spirit empowers the church to continue Jesus' mission. Through the pouring out of the Spirit at Pentecost, the disciples were formed into a Spirit-filled community through which God would work to rescue and renew the world.

The mission of Jesus was to regather and restore Israel—his "little flock"—and then send it to the nations so they could be incorporated into the people of God. That was the promise of the prophets throughout the Old Testament. Now that regathered "flock" is being commissioned, empowered, and sent. Jesus' mission to Israel is to be the model for their mission to the nations.

To summarize what we saw in the previous section, Jesus' own mission looked something like this:

- Jesus proclaimed God's kingdom and called people to enter the kingdom community by faith and repentance ("repent and believe the good news") and to receive its blessings and take up its demands.
- Through the Spirit's power, Jesus demonstrated the reign of God, beginning to reverse the consequences of embedded evil and to restore human life to the *shalom* that God originally intended.

- Jesus formed a visible and identifiable community called to be a contrast society—the vision for which was laid out in the Sermon on the Mount (Matt. 5–7; cf. Lk. 6:17–46).
- Jesus was the True Human, and his own life demonstrated life under God's reign: one on whom the Spirit rested, one with an intimate "*Abba*" relationship with the Father, one with a deep life of prayer focused on the coming of the kingdom.
- Jesus identified with the poor, marginalized, and outcast people of his time, inviting them to his table to participate in the feast of the kingdom; indeed, preaching the gospel to such people is a sign of the kingdom (Lk. 7:22).
- Jesus' mission was characterized by compassion, justice, generosity, joy, forgiveness, and holding possessions lightly (Lk. 6:24–26; 12:13–21; 19:1–10).
- Jesus' challenge to the prevailing order of Israel and of Rome—especially the "gods" that sanctioned Roman culture—brought opposition and suffering; and he is clear that disciples should expect suffering as the normal result of discipleship (John 15:18–20).[5]

At Pentecost the church was commissioned to continue this mission. The exalted Christ poured out the Spirit for this very purpose. The Holy Spirit is the Spirit of Jesus Christ; the Spirit's mission is to continue the mission of Christ. The Spirit represents Christ, always points to Christ, and draws people to Christ. And we can be confident that mission empowered by the Spirit is always consistent with the person and mission of Christ.

The outpouring of the Spirit empowers witness to God's reign and the spread of "new creation." The resurrected Jesus tells his questioning disciples that they will be his witnesses "when the Holy Spirit comes upon you" (Acts 1:7–8). The background is Isaiah 43:1–12 and other New Exodus prophecies (Isa. 40–55) envisioning that in the age to come, the people of Israel will become witnesses to all the nations of God's great salvation. The nations assemble and say,

Let them bring in their witnesses to prove they were right,

so that others may hear and say, "It is true."
"You are my witnesses," declares the LORD,
    "and my servant whom I have chosen,
so that you may know and believe me
    and understand that I am he.
Before me no god was formed,
    nor will there be one after me."

"You are my witnesses," declares the LORD, "that I am God."
(Isa. 43:9b–10, 12)

These prophecies were now fulfilled. The age of salvation, accomplished in Christ and present through the Spirit, had burst on the scene. And the disciples became witnesses.

The outpouring of the Spirit empowers the apostles to preach about Jesus, indeed to become prophets like Jesus, including the working of "signs and wonders." But the falling of the Spirit is not limited to the apostles; the Spirit is poured out on "all flesh": "your sons and your daughters shall prophesy, and your young men shall see visions, and your old men shall dream dreams." And even more, "Even upon my slaves, both men and women, I will pour out my Spirit in those days ; and they will prophecy" (Acts 2:17–18, quoting Joel 2:28–9).

This first apostolic witness was in some ways unique and unrepeatable, but the role of witness was not limited to the apostles. Witness becomes the calling of the church. All are empowered by the Spirit to take up Jesus' proclamation of liberty to the captives. It is the work of the Spirit to make witnesses (*martyres*). Stephen was a witness when his sermon provoked his martyrdom. As the stones came down, he received a Spirit-given vision of Jesus in glory that became his public witness, sealed by his blood (Acts 7).

The Spirit guides and empowers the Christian mission. In Acts, the Spirit is mentioned fifty-nine times. The Spirit inspires bold proclamation and focused teaching about Jesus. The filling of the Spirit enables Peter to proclaim salvation in Jesus' name to the elders and teachers of the law (Acts 4:8–12). Stephen, a man "full of faith and of the Holy Spirit," was chosen to serve the Grecian widows and empowered by the Spirit to proclaim a broader vision of God's purposes through Israel (6:5–10). And Saul of Tarsus, after Jesus appeared to him in a vision and he was left blind, was visited by Ananias who laid his hands on him and said, "The Lord . . . has sent me so that you may see again and be filled with the Holy Spirit"; the result was that "at once he began to preach in the synagogues that Jesus is the Son of God" (Acts 9:17, 20). In the story of Acts, the Spirit chooses missionaries ("the Holy Spirit said, 'Set apart for me Barnabas and Saul,'" 13:2), and opens and closes doors (keeping the apostles out of Asia, 16:6–7, and urging Paul not to go to Rome, 21:4).

All the way through the story of the early church's mission and expansion in Acts, the role of the Spirit can hardly be exaggerated: "the church is above all else the locus of the Spirit; her origin, direction, authority, expansion, and development are directly the Spirit's concern, and her members are those upon on whom the Spirit has 'fallen' or 'been poured.'"[6]

That mission is a dynamic process in which the Spirit is at work in believers, the body of Christ, to bear witness to the saving and liberating work of Jesus Christ for all nations. The Spirit is the power of the creator God and the Spirit of the resurrected Messiah. And his disciples are invited, in the power of the Spirit, to participate in this cosmic work.

The Spirit enables the church to follow the sacrificial path of Jesus. Just as Jesus ministered through the anointing of the Spirit and poured himself out through the empowerment of the Spirit, so his disciples, in a similar way, receive the Spirit's anointing and empowerment to become a community of sacrificial caring that serves as a sign and means of the coming of God's kingdom.

And discipleship in this way of Jesus will involve contradiction and weariness. In Acts, the mission propelled by the Spirit involves opposition, challenges, and suffering at every turn. That appears to be the way the reign of God comes—through the way of Jesus, which is the way of sacrificial love.

The period between Pentecost and the return of Christ can be called the age of the Holy Spirit. It is the time when the Spirit disperses the church throughout the world with the mandate to call people to believe the gospel, repent, and live under God's reign.

Jesus said he would send "another Advocate" to be with the disciples forever (John 14:16). The Advocate, he says, will "testify about me" (15:26). The Advocate bears witness to Jesus, and Jesus bears witness to the Father. The Spirit exalts Christ and empowers witness to him. That is the key mission of the Spirit. We honor the Spirit, not when we hear much about the Spirit, but when we hear much about Christ. The Spirit doesn't bear witness to the Spirit.

The Trinity-in-Mission

The Spirit has tended to be squeezed out of an integral and equal role with the Son in God's mission. Recovery is needed. The mission of the Spirit, I have affirmed, is equal in importance to the mission of the Son. The Spirit is not a junior partner in the Trinity.

What does this mean? It means a deeply reciprocal and intimate relationship between Christ and the Spirit. By the Spirit Jesus was conceived, anointed, commissioned, empowered, sustained, and raised from the dead. By Christ, after his ascension and exaltation, the Spirit was "poured out" to empower and guide Christ's continuing mission. Jesus was a man of the Spirit, and the Spirit became the "Spirit of Christ." Christ was the central focus of the mission of the Spirit; the Spirit became the key agent of the mission of Christ.

We can say that there was a double sending—two missions: the mission of the Spirit and the mission of the Son. The Father sends both the Son and the Spirit. Thus Galatians 4:4–6 indicates: "God sent his Son. . . . God has sent the Spirit of his Son." John's Gospel also speaks of this double mission (7:37–39; 14:26; 20:21–22).

Paul's use of the important phrases "in Christ" and "in the Spirit" reveals the deep mutuality between Christ and the Spirit in carrying out the Father's mission. Being "in Christ" means, for Paul, always being "in the Spirit." The two phrases are virtually interchangeable. In a key passage, Paul declares that Christians are "in the Spirit" and that "anyone who does not have the Spirit of Christ does not belong to Christ" (Rom. 8:9). Further, God has "anointed us . . . and put his Spirit in our hearts as a deposit, guaranteeing what is to come" (2 Cor. 1:2122). When one is united with Christ,

107

the Spirit becomes the sphere in which the Christian lives. To be "in Christ" is to be "in the Spirit."

Christ is the message and focus of the gospel. The Spirit constantly lifts up Christ and shines the spotlight on him, always enabling him to be the center of the gospel. The very truth about Christ—that he is God in the flesh, Son, Savior, and Messiah—becomes intelligible through the deep work of the Spirit. "The Spirit searches all things, even the deep things of God," says Paul; and we have received "the Spirit who is from God, that we may understand what God has freely given us" (1 Cor. 2:10b, 12). "No one can say, 'Jesus is Lord' except by the Holy Spirit" (1 Cor. 12:3). In John's writings as well, we see a way of knowing by the Spirit that is part of the normal life of the Christian community: "this is how we know that he [Christ] lives in us: We know it by the Spirit he gave us" (1 John 3:24; see also 4:13).

The mission of the Son becomes operative and effective through the mission of the Spirit. This is how the Trinity-in-mission operates. God reaches through the Son in the Spirit to reconcile and transform, and leads people in the Spirit through the Son back to the Father. This is the movement, the proportionality, of the Trinity. In this movement, the missions of the Son and of the Spirit are equal, each according to its distinct function.

What does this mean for our preaching and teaching? Does it mean we give equal time to equal missions? Do we place half our focus on Jesus the Son and half on the Spirit? Do we preach Pentecost and the Spirit as central to the gospel? Do we give equal space in our theology books to the Son and to the Spirit?

We do what the apostles did after the Spirit was poured out at Pentecost: we proclaim Christ and him crucified; we proclaim that Christ "died for our sins in accordance with the Scripture and was raised on the third day"; we declare that the very person of Jesus—empowered by the Spirit—embodied the presence of God's reign. We declare, as Paul said, "the mystery of God, namely, Christ, in whom are hidden all the treasures of wisdom and knowledge" (Col. 2:2–3). The New Testament does not make the Holy Spirit the central content of the gospel. The first missionaries did not proclaim the Holy Spirit; they proclaimed Christ—as Messiah, Lord, redeemer, sin-bearer, and victor.

But still, the Spirit is not the junior partner, though the Christian tradition has often treated the Spirit that way. The words of Kilian McDonnell—which could almost be a poem—capture the distinctiveness yet equality and mutuality of the two missions:

> Without the mission of the Spirit what is left of faith and experience are the dried structural bones of religion. Liturgy is ceremony and ritual, prayer is formula, theology is the proposition of ideology that excites and changes no one. . . . Without the mission of the Spirit no one can grasp the hem of the Son's garment. . . .
>
> [But] Without the mission of the Son the mission of the Spirit is devoid of the flesh and materiality that make salvation history possible. Without the mission of the Son the mission of the Spirit floats above time, looking for flesh it can touch and transform. . . . Without the mission of the Son the church is a mystical illusion, shadows upon the wall.
>
> [So the] two missions [of Christ and the Spirit] are not separate. Cannot be divorced. Each is present at the interior of the other, a deep calling unto deep, light illuminating light, witnessing to the love of the Father, bending over the world with troubled love, gathering humanity and the universe with the two divine arms, the Son and the Spirit, into the untroubled glory that is the ultimate consummation of all.[7]

Here is a broad and beautiful vision of the Trinity-in-mission.

I turn next to look at two key aspects of the Spirit: empowering for mission and bestowing gifts for mission.

The Empowering Spirit

Paul understands the Spirit as experiential empowerment in the community of faith. When Paul engages the Galatians about the place of works of law, an essential part of his argument is from experience: "Did you receive the Spirit by works of the law, or by believing what you heard? . . . Have you experienced so much in vain?" (Gal. 3:2, 4). Paul assumes rather than argues for the dynamic presence of the Spirit. He assumes that his readers were all made alive by the Spirit (3:14), received birth by the Spirit (4:29), experienced miracles by the Spirit (3:4–5), received the experience of sonship through the Spirit (4:5–7), and through the Spirit have entered into new creation—and "a new creation is everything" (6:15). The coming of the Spirit was, for Paul, an identifiable event experienced in the community as empowerment and attested in a variety of ways.

Though the Spirit is present in power at conversion, Paul also exhorts believers to "be filled with the Spirit" or to "keep on being filled with the Spirit" (Eph. 5:18). The Ephesian disciples are already a temple of the Holy Spirit, but Paul nonetheless tells them that "you too are being built together to become a dwelling in which God lives by his Spirit" (Eph. 2:22). The Spirit already dwells in the church, yet the church still needs further filling with the Spirit.

How can those who are already baptized in the Spirit need and receive further filling? How can we best think about the ongoing process of being filled with the Spirit?

Being "filled with the Spirit" is a metaphor describing ongoing receptivity to the Spirit. Just as the Spirit has been "poured out," so the community and individual disciples can be "filled" with the Spirit. To be filled with the Spirit is to come under more intense and intimate influence of the Spirit. The Spirit's filling can be diminished—quenched—and subsequently experienced again, on multiple occasions, throughout a Christian's life. Disciples can be "filled with the Spirit" to enable them to perform a special task or to equip them for service or ministry. Paul also speaks about "God's provision of the Spirit" (Phil. 1:19) in facing hardship. Especially in the throes of mission, disciples can experience God's love and empowering presence in a fuller, more intense way ("strengthened with might through his Spirit in your inner being," Eph. 3:16).

Because the Spirit is present and active in the body of Christ as well as in our own individual "temples," we can experience new fillings of the Spirit, sometimes bringing deep healing to our lives, sometimes stirring fresh new joy and peace, sometimes lighting the fire of mission within us, sometimes sustaining us under heavy burdens. And there is a biblical rubric to guide us in our experience of the Spirit. It is for the "common good." It is for mission. "This is how you ascertain the truth of spiritual experience," advised Christian Wiman, whose own faith was reborn on the long road of illness: "it propels you back toward the world and other people, and not simply more deeply within yourself."[8]

For Paul, the terms "Spirit" and "power" are sometimes nearly inter-changeable, as in 1 Corinthians 2 ("demonstration of the Spirit and of power," v. 4; cf. 1 Thess. 1:5). This power is the source of "signs and won-ders" (Gal. 3:5) and "full conviction" (1 Thess. 1:5). But this power is that of a particular sort. It is the power of cruciform love. "In 1 Corinthians Paul makes the combination of cruciformity and power the test for all claims to possession of the Spirit."[9] The Spirit empowers believers to serve and edify in the way of Jesus, which is self-giving love—a love ultimately defined by the cross. Without this love as the fundamental reality, the Spirit's empow-erment avails little (13:1–3).

The Charismatic Spirit

One clear way this empowerment was manifested was through the variety of grace-gifts that were active in the church, a variety that may be seen in the lists that Paul gives in 1 Corinthians and Romans. "There are varieties of gifts, but the same Spirit; and there are varieties of services, but the same Lord; and there are varieties of activities, but the same God who activates all of them in everyone. To each is given the manifestation of the Spirit for the common good" (1 Cor. 12:4–7 ESV).

Only rarely does Paul speak of the Spirit in individual terms (1 Cor. 7:40; maybe 14:14). He normally speaks of "you" and "us" (Rom. 5:5; 7:6; 8:9, 11, 15, 23, 26). He speaks of the *"fellowship* of the Holy Spirit" (2 Cor. 13:14). In 1 Corinthians 12:13, the one body is a function of their common experi-ence of the one Spirit—"one Spirit, therefore one body." For Paul, the shared experience of the Spirit was fundamental to the Christian community.

According to Paul, membership in the one body of Christ meant charis-matic membership (1 Cor. 12:4–11, 27–30). Each member has his or her own gift—no one is lacking the Spirit's gifts of grace (Rom. 12:4–8; 1 Cor. 7:7).

111

The *charismata* or grace-gifts are richly varied and are given for the sake of the "common good," for building up the body (12:7). Paul's gift lists are only ad hoc illustrations of the great diversity of gifts. In 1 Corinthians 12–14 we find seven such lists (12:8–10; 12:28, 29–30; 13:1–3, 8; 14:6, 26), and they show considerable diversity in language and character. In Romans 12:6–8 Paul includes a somewhat different list. Clearly he does not have a set number in mind but views the Spirit's gifts in the body as widely diverse.

God's grace-gifts, indeed, were experienced in every sphere of the community's life and were not limited to the phenomena described in 1 Corinthians 12–14. Note the way Paul expands the doctrine of the *charismata* to the range of circumstances in which believers find themselves. Defending his own celibacy, Paul regards the capacity to remain unmarried and avoid sexual temptation as a *charisma*. "But each of you has your own gift from God; one has this gift, another has that" (1 Cor. 7:7). So, whether married or unmarried, slave or free, circumcised or uncircumcised, God's gracious gifts are given in each life circumstance. Paul longs to go to Rome so that he can "impart to you some spiritual gift to make you strong" (Rom. 1:11).

When members refuse to acknowledge and exercise the Spirit's gift, they "quench" the Spirit and, in the process, cease to function as members of the body (1 Thess. 5:19). Paul does not conceive of two kinds of Christians—charismatics and noncharismatics, those who have grace-gifts to serve the body and those who don't, those who minister to others and those who only receive ministry. "To be Christian," James Dunn asserts, summarizing Paul, "is to be charismatic; one cannot be a member of the body without sharing the charismatic Spirit."[10] Paul does not envision passive membership in the body of Christ; to be baptized into Christ through the Spirit means initiation into active, Spirit-gifted membership (1 Cor. 12:13).

Paul also recognizes that the mere claim to the possession of the Spirit's gift is not evidence that one has the gift. Indeed, in 2 Corinthians he must counter the charge that he is not a man of the Spirit. Opponents have made an impressive case, based on their own gifts and ecstatic experience, that they, and not Paul, possess the Spirit. Paul counters their claims by an appeal to his weakness as the demonstration of the power of God in his own ministry. Paul clearly knows that the claim of experience is not final evidence that one possesses the Spirit. Indeed, God's power can work through human weakness so that the power of the Holy Spirit is not self-evident to many observers.

So the community of the Spirit faces the necessary matter of "discerning the spirits." "Do not despise prophecies but test everything" (1 Thess. 5:20–21 ESV), says Paul. His criteria for discernment are laid out most clearly in 1 Corinthians 12–14:

- Confession of Jesus as Lord (12:3)
- Love (13)
- Building up the community of faith (14:3–5, 12, 17, 26)

The key for Paul was his identification of the Spirit as the "Spirit of Christ." So the Spirit always shapes believers more and more into the image and likeness of Christ (2 Cor. 3:18), and always produces the fruit of Christ-like character (Gal. 5:22–23). And this image of Christ is not only of the *exalted* Christ, for "as soon as a charismatic experience becomes an experience only of the exalted Christ and not also of the crucified Jesus, it loses its distinctive Christian character."[11] The Spirit of joy and fullness is also the Spirit of self-sacrificing mission.

For Paul the ultimate criterion for discerning the Spirit's activity was not the presence of power and gifts, but rather the confession and lifting up of Jesus as Lord. The criterion for the exercise of the Spirit's gifts is their use in a way that enables people to see and enter God's kingdom. They are gifts for mission. Anything less than that "begins to move away from Christ to a more pagan fascination with spiritual activity as an end in itself."[12] James Dunn adds, "For Paul *charisma* never amounted to anything unless it expressed the *charis*, the grace of God manifested most clearly in Christ."[13]

For Paul the already/not yet framework is the fundamental way of understanding the Spirit's work; through the Spirit, God's promised end time is already breaking into the present. The reign of God is breaking in, and "new creation" is breaking out. But the sense of that inbreaking in the power of the Spirit eventually diminished in the Christian tradition. The

Spirit and eschatology were separated. The Spirit's end-time work in the church was minimized, and the "new creation" effects of Jesus' victory were mostly postponed to the future promise of heaven.

What also diminished along with the end-time orientation was the universality of *charisma*, the every-member giftedness by which each one ministered to the common good of the one body and participated in God's mission. In the Christendom centuries, the "clergy" ministered to a mostly passive "laity." As Emil Brunner put it, "the Ecclesia became a dispensing entity rather than a ministering fellowship."[14] Now, after Christendom, the New Testament's every-member-giftedness and the diversity of the Spirit's gifts are becoming a larger possibility. How? "The Christian church will be open for the diversity of the Spirit's gifts . . . to the degree in which it wins back its original eschatological orientation towards the [inbreaking] new creation."[15]

With the functioning of Christ's gifts to the body, Paul envisions it "attaining to the whole measure of the fullness of Christ"; disciples will thereby "grow up" into Christ and the body "grows and builds itself up in love, as each part does its work" (Eph. 4:13, 15–16).

The Receding and Recovery of Mission

The diminishment of the eschatological role of the Spirit (the inbreaking of God's future) and of the church as a "fellowship of the Holy Spirit" in the Christendom centuries was paralleled by the receding of mission as a defining mark and dynamic feature of the church. With this characterization I don't mean to deny or downplay the rich traditions of monasticism, mystical spirituality, and the spiritual writers of Christendom. Many spiritual giants worked within the structures of the Christendom church, many of them seeking to evangelize, renew, and reform. But I am saying that the predominant focus on the Spirit in the Christendom centuries was inward, mystical, and pietistic, with little emphasis on the Spirit as the power of Christ's mission to the nations—which seems to be the New Testament focus.

Christendom was a cultural system in which Christian faith was maintained by law, indeed by coercion. The church joined forces with the state to ensure that the entire population was both church members and citizens.

In the context of Christendom, the place of mission was greatly diminished. The whole society, by definition, was Christian, and so the church as a missionary presence simply didn't make sense. The missionary calling as an inherent part of the nature of the church receded.

This is not to say that the missional movement disappeared. From about the fourth century through the fifteenth century, new monastic movements kept mission alive, mostly around the margins of Christendom. As Christendom culture spread, monasteries became missional outposts among largely unconverted peoples. They brought Christian witness, education, and care for the poor. Through their efforts, the pagan tribes of Europe were gradually evangelized and then assimilated into European culture. St. Patrick (d. 493 AD), missionary to Ireland, became one of the best-known leaders of the monastic mission movement. Large numbers of the pagan Celts were converted, and monastic outposts were established in Ireland, Scotland, and parts of England.

But as Christendom spread and the church became wealthy, monasticism itself faced strong corrupting forces, wealth and comfort chief among them. There also emerged new orders of militant monks, like the Knights Templars (early twelfth century), who sought to spread the faith with the sword in the crusades and beyond. Beginning around the fifteenth century, the popes authorized the Spanish and Portuguese crowns to send expeditions of conquest to the Americas, and these expeditions included chaplains to provide pastoral care of the Europeans and to do mission work among the "heathen." Mission was directed only to people beyond the borders of Christendom, where the faith was often propagated by some degree of coercion.

"The Constantinian relationship," John Yoder noted, "represents a fundamental shift away from the nature of the church as mission-oriented."[16] In the Christendom context, the church gets increasingly defined as an institution dispensing grace and providing pastoral care to the "Christian" masses. It helps maintain proper order in society, provides spiritual aid and comfort in the struggles of life, and serves as an ark or fortress in which Christians are protected. It is a static and institutional conception of the church. The focus is inward, not outward.

My key point in this complex story is this: With the receding of the church's mission orientation, the doctrine of the Spirit was constricted, now redefined by the settled caretaker role that the empire required. The loss of mission corresponds to a narrowed and tamed doctrine of the Spirit. The two diminishments go hand in hand.

This static conception of the church remained in the churches of the Protestant Reformation as well. The Augsburg Confession (1530) of the early Lutheran movement set out two basic marks of the church: "The Church is the congregation of the saints in which the Gospel is purely taught, and the sacraments are rightly administered." The Thirty-Nine Articles of the Anglican Church followed suit: "The visible Church of Christ is a congregation of faithful men, in which the pure Word of God is preached, and the Sacraments be duly administered according to Christ's ordinances. . . ." In these classic Protestant formulations, focus falls on the *being* of the church, not its *function*. It is defined as "a place where something is done, not a living organism doing something."[17]

The Protestant churches remained firmly situated within Christendom, and there was little sense that the church was an instrument of Christ's continuing, Spirit-empowered and guided mission to the world. Indeed, the early Reformers flatly rejected any missionary duty for the churches. In the context of a Christendom Europe controlled by the Catholic Church, they sought to reform the church so that it was a proper place for preaching the Word and celebrating the sacraments—not so it would be a Spirit-empowered movement to embody and proclaim God's *shalom* to the nations.

Since that time, as a legacy of Christendom, mission has tended to remain secondary or even peripheral to the vision of the church in the West. The missionary movement of the nineteenth century took place largely in mission societies outside the institutional churches of late Christendom. As the nineteenth century progressed, these mission societies stirred renewal among the established churches, though theologically "mission" continued to remain mostly separated from "church."

As we saw in Chapter Two, it was among the sixteenth-century Radicals that the church was defined as essentially missional. To the two defining Protestant marks (preaching the gospel and rightly observing the sacraments), they added four more: holy living, discipleship, witness (missionary vitality), and the cross (suffering).[18] They could do this because they had broken with Christendom and found themselves very quickly in a perilously missional situation. All across Europe they became pilgrims and exiles, witnesses and martyrs. They experienced a whole new meaning of the church as a "fellowship of the Holy Spirit." I don't mean to idealize the Radicals; they had their own issues and deficiencies. But they did recover, in the most searing of circumstances, a fundamental element—discipleship of Christ in the power of the Spirit—that had been generally diminished in the Christendom centuries.

With the devastating wars of (Christian) religion in seventeenth-century Europe and the emergence of the humanistic Enlightenment, where Christian faith was steadily pressured and privatized, Christendom steadily receded in the West.

By the mid-twentieth century, Western Christendom—in decline and decay for many generations—had virtually collapsed. In 1949 historian Herbert Butterfield noted the remarkable fact that, for the first time in about fifteen centuries, no person in the West was being compelled by government to call himself or herself Christian.[19] By the 1960s in America, the "third disestablishment" of the church from its once dominant place in American culture was underway with the cultural revolution of that decade.[20] By late century David Bosch could observe that the collapse of Christendom—though many lamented its passing—had actually liberated the church, stripping it of its earlier self-confidence, assumptions of power, and comfortable chaplain's role. Now the church could, once again, more truly be the church. It could recover its essential missional character—and "the intrinsic missionary character of the Holy Spirit." It could be modeled after its Servant Lord, and mission could become "the church-crossing-borders-in-the-form-of-a-servant."[21]

It is noteworthy and not surprising that, with the collapse of Christendom, the deeply ensconced Christendom churches themselves began to rethink and renew the focus on God's mission. For the Roman Catholic Church, the Second Vatican Council in the early 1960s brought a new and vigorous focus on "the missionary activity of the church located in Trinitarian *missio Dei*," and with this focus—also as one would expect—new emphasis on the Holy Spirit of mission. Thus some could speak of the council as pointing toward a "new Pentecost." And Pope Paul VI could acknowledge the Catholic charismatic renewal, which began in the sixties, as a gift to the church. About the same time, Karl Rahner, a leading Catholic theologian, asserted that "Christendom is going to disappear with ever-increasing speed" and that Christian faith will exist more and more as diaspora or exile communities around the world.[22]

"With the collapse of historical Christendom," Wilbert Shenk said, "the church today is a minority in most countries. To be viable the church must assume a *missionary* relationship to every culture. . . . The church dare not make the mistake of thinking that it must gain control of society in order to proclaim the gospel. God has not called the church to govern the world but to witness to God's plan to renew the world based on the justice/righteousness of God."[23] On God's mission the stance is not dominance and control, but witness, patience, and (often) suffering—all sustained by the ministry and empowerment of the Holy Spirit.

The cross of Christ remains our model for the renewal of mission, cutting through humanity's persistent and natural tendency to dominate and impose. Christ himself, in the power of the Spirit, "taking the form of a servant. . . humbled himself and became obedient to the point of death—even death on a cross" (Phil. 2:7–8 ESV). That is also the posture sought by his disciples in their mission—a daunting and unnatural posture, but one that we grow steadily into as we apply ourselves to formation by the Spirit in Christ's community, as we will see in the next chapter.

NOTES

[1] Christopher J. H. Wright, *The Mission of God: Unlocking the Bible's Grand Narrative* (Downers Grove, IL: InterVarsity, 2006), 470. Also rich and helpful in tracing this story through Scripture is Michael Goheen, *A Light to the Nations: The Missional Church and the Biblical Story* (Grand Rapids: Baker Academic, 2011).

[2] Perry Yoder, *Shalom: The Bible's Word for Salvation* (Nappanee, IN: Evangel, 1998).

[3] N. T. Wright, *The Day the Revolution Began: Reconsidering the Meaning of Jesus' Crucifixion* (New York: HarperOne, 2016), 85–86.

[4] Richard Hays, *The Moral Vision of the New Testament: A Contemporary Introduction to New Testament Ethics* (New York: HarperCollins, 1996), 201.

[5] This summary follows loosely that of Goheen, *A Light to the Nations*, 118.

[6] R. E. O. White, *The Biblical Doctrine of Initiation* (Grand Rapids: Eerdmans, 1960), 189.

[7] Kilian McDonnell, *The Other Hand of God* (Collegeville, MN: Liturgical Press, 2003), 228, 229.

[8] Christian Wiman, *My Bright Abyss: Meditations of a Modern Believer* (New York: Farrar, Strauss & Giroux, 2013), 75.

[9] Gorman, *Cruciformity: Paul's Narrative Spirituality of the Cross* (Grand Rapids: Eerdmans, 2001), 59.

[10] James D. G. Dunn, *Jesus and the Spirit: A Study of the Religious and Charismatic Experience of Jesus and the First Christians as Reflected in the New Testament* (Grand Rapids: Eerdmans, 1997), 264.

[11] Dunn, Jesus and the Spirit, 331.

[12] Gordon Fee, *God's Empowering Presence: The Holy Spirit in the Letters of Paul* (Peabody, MA: Hendrickson, 1994), 158.

[13] James D. G. Dunn, "Towards the Spirit of Christ: The Emergence of the Distinctive Features of Christian Pneumatology," in *The Work of the Spirit*, ed. Michael Welker (Grand Rapids: Eerdmans, 2006), 25.

[14] Emil Brunner, *Dogmatics, Volume 3: The Christian Doctrine of the Church, Faith and the Consummation* (London: Lutterworth, 1962), 45.

[15] Jürgen Moltmann, *The Church in the Power of the Spirit* (New York: Harper & Row, 1977), 299.

[16] John Yoder, *Theology of Mission: A Believers Church Perspective* (Downers Grove, IL: InterVarsity, 2014), 177.

[17] David Bosch, *Transforming Mission: Paradigm Shifts in the Theology of Mission*, 20th anniversary edition (1991; Orbis, 2011), 249.

[18] *Complete Writings of Menno Simons, 1496–1561*, trans. Leonard Verduin and ed. John Wenger (Scottdale, PA: Herald, 1956), 739–44.

[19] Herbert Butterfield, *Christianity and History* (London: Bell & Sons, 1949), 135.

[20] Phillip E. Hammond, *Religion and Personal Autonomy: The Third Disestablishment in America* (Columbia, SC: University of South Carolina, 1992).

[21] Bosch, *Transforming Mission*, 116, and *Witness to the World* (Eugene, OR: Wipf and Stock, 1980), 248.

[22] Thomas Hughson, "Interpreting Vatican II: 'A New Pentecost,'" *Theological Studies* 69 (2008): 35; Karl Rahner, "Christians in the Modern World," in *The Christian Commitment* (New York: Sheed & Ward, 1963), 17–18.

[23] Wilbert Shenk, "New Wineskins for New Wine: Towards a Post-Christendom Ecclesiology," *International Bulletin of Missionary Research* 29 (April 2005): 77. Though professed Christians are clearly not a minority in the United States, the character of the United States as a "Christian" nation has clearly changed. As Walter Brueggemann has said, "if it be insisted that church members are still in places of social power and influence, I suggest that such Christians only need to act and speak out of any serious conviction concerning the public claims of the gospel, and it becomes promptly evident that we are outsiders to the flow of power." *The Word Militant: Preaching a Decentering Word* (Philadelphia: Fortress, 2007), 133.

FORMATION

The Spirit, through faith and attendance to the means of grace, forms us into the image of Jesus Christ.

The Spirit's work is centered on enabling the ordinary, and especially ordinary life in the human body, to be what it is made to be.
—Colin Gunton

The church's worship is a uniquely intense site of the Spirit's transformative presence.
—James K. A. Smith

The Christian life, for Paul, begins by faith in the crucified Christ and the powerfully effective gift of the Spirit. When Paul reminds believers of their conversion to Christ, he normally points them to the role played by the Spirit. The Spirit enabled them to declare that Jesus is Lord; the Spirit poured God's love into their hearts (Rom. 5:5); the Spirit brought about their adoption as sons and daughters, enabling them to enter into an *Abba* relationship with the Father (Gal. 4:6; Rom. 8:15).

Paul worries that the Galatian Christians, having begun with the Spirit, are turning back to human effort and thus negating their rich experience of the Spirit (Gal. 3:1–3). It is through the Spirit alone, not through Torah-keeping, that they can reach their goal. What is that goal? It is for Christ to be formed in them (Gal. 4:19). The goal of the Christian life is to be conformed to the image of the Son (Rom. 8:29; 2 Cor. 3:18).

Paul attributes the deep transformation of our lives to the work of the Spirit. How does that happen? Are we passive receptacles for the Spirit? Do we need to do anything? How does the Spirit form us into the image of Christ?

Let's begin with a four-part definition of Christian formation: "our continuing response to the reality of God's grace shaping us into the likeness of Jesus Christ, through the work of the Holy Spirit, in the community of faith, for the sake of the world."[1] Into the likeness of Christ. Through the Spirit. In the community of faith. For the sake of the world. In this chapter, I focus on these four deeply intertwined realities.

Befriending the Body

It may seem like an odd place to start, but I think it necessary to make this affirmation: Christian formation is inescapably physical and bodily, not just intellectual and mystical.

The Christian tradition, especially in the modern period in the West, has tended to embrace what we can call a spirit-matter dualism. It goes back to Plato's sharp dualism, and has been deeply woven into the Christian tradition. Material things are shadowlike, insubstantial, and impermanent, always tumbling toward decay; the soul or spirit is immortal, not subject to the ravages of time upon matter. So materiality, and physical existence, is to be transcended, the soul released from its earthly constraints. Souls were meant to live in the nonmaterial, eternal realm.

In the modern period this spirit-matter dualism took a new form that we can call mind-body dualism. Charles Taylor calls it "excarnation." Incarnation—a centerpiece of the Christian faith—means "enfleshment," the full embrace of the bodily and the physical; excarnation means "defleshment," a separation of the bodily from the immaterial mind. Taylor describes it as "the exaltation of the disengaged reason as the royal road to knowledge."[2] The predominant assumption of the Enlightenment has been that we live in an impersonal universe governed by unbending natural laws, and that such a world is best studied and mastered by "disengaged reason"—that is, with as little interference as possible by the messy particularities of one's humanity. Reason, logic, and argument—functions of the mind—supersede the truths of the body, of feelings, habits, and practices. The body becomes a mode of transport for the mind/soul, simply part of the objectified natural world governed by laws of nature.

This disengagement of mind from body is paralleled by a split between the natural and the supernatural. God tends to become—for many of those who continue to believe in God—a distant architect of a world governed by unchanging natural laws. This means that the supernatural must interrupt or shock nature. So miracles become "a kind of punctual hole blown in the regular order of things from the outside."[3] They become rare—and maybe even extinct—occurrences. The dualism of matter-spirit and body-mind contrasts sharply with the world of the biblical story.

First, the physical world, including human bodies, is good. God's love affair with matter began in Genesis, when God created this world and said it was "very good." Creation, to be sure, is disordered or "fallen" in the biblical view but still permeated by signs of grace and beauty—because creation is "good." C. S. Lewis reminds us not to try to be more spiritual than God. "God likes matter. He invented it."[4] And it will continue into eternity with the Creator's promise of a new heaven and a new earth. God is redeeming and renewing the creation, and the people of God, in the power of the Spirit, are already an advance guard of the new heavens and new earth.

Second, Spirit is not opposed to material things and to human bodies; in Scripture, beginning in the Old Testament (with wind, breath, spirit—all one Hebrew word), Spirit has a "positive relationship to all creation, the 'material' and the 'spiritual' alike."[5] In Psalm 104, a creation psalm, God's Spirit presides over the living material world: "when you take away their breath, they die and return to the dust. When you send your Spirit, they are created, and you renew the face of the earth" (104:29b–30). In the Hebrew view, humans are not immortal souls incarnated (even trapped) in physical bodies; rather, they are spirited bodies—"complex physical organisms . . . blown by the Breath of God's Spirit."[6]

God's Spirit is not only the Spirit of a "spiritual" part of humans but the Spirit of every dimension of life. This frail and mortal body, says Paul, becomes "the temple of the Holy Spirit." And further, the body is meant "for the Lord, and the Lord for the body" (1 Cor. 6:13 ESV). So he admonishes disciples to "glorify God in your body." The Spirit brings life and new creation, not ghostlike escape from the world. "The Spirit does not draw the soul away from the body, nor does it make the soul hasten towards heaven, leaving this earth behind. It places the whole earthly and bodily person in the daybreak colors of the new earth. That is why Paul can describe the raising of the dead as 'giving life to our mortal bodies' (Rom. 8:11)."[7]

Third, at the heart of the gospel is the incarnation of Christ. The Son of God becomes a human being. He is enfleshed and so "befriends" the physical body—all the way from conception in the womb of Mary to bodily resurrection from the dead and indeed to the final judgment. Reflecting Christ's incarnation, Christian faith, properly understood, is thoroughly *incarnational*. Incarnation teaches us that the Creator loves the stuff of creation.

Jesus' resurrection was of his body, a fulfillment of God's creational intent in making human beings. Paul makes this point in 1 Corinthians 15: the resurrection will not be a disembodiment but a new and fuller embodiment. Jesus was the firstborn from the dead but remained bodily human, and by his resurrection became a promise of resurrection to others (1 Cor. 15:42–53). The Lord Jesus will "transform our lowly bodies so that they will be like his glorious body" (Phil. 3:21). The "spiritual body" of the age to come will not be a dematerialized body in a dematerialized world, but rather a Spirit-quickened, hyperphysical body dwelling in a "new creation" filled with the glory and presence of God.[8]

Fourth, Scripture reveals the intimate relationship between Jesus and the Spirit. At the annunciation, the angel says to Mary, "The Holy Spirit will come upon you, and the power of the Most High will overshadow you" (Lk. 1:35a). At his baptism, the Spirit came to rest or dwell on Jesus in bodily form like a dove (Lk. 3:21). Full of the Spirit and led by the Spirit into the desert, he was tempted for forty days (Lk. 4:1). Under the anointing of the Spirit, Jesus "went around doing good and healing all who were under the power of the devil" (Acts 10:38). And following the crucifixion, God with the Holy Spirit raised Jesus' body from the dead (Rom. 8:11).

Here we see the close relationship between the Spirit and the Son in the incarnation. Jesus took on flesh and became a human being. And the Spirit was with him every step of the way. At Jesus' baptism, the Spirit comes to rest on his body. We might say that the Spirit, for the sake of the beloved Jesus, became a friend of the physical body. "To think about the Spirit," says Eugene Rogers, "you have to think materially because, in Christian terms, the Spirit has befriended matter. She has befriended matter for Christ's sake on account of the incarnation."[9] And at Pentecost the Spirit came to rest on Christ's body once again—his body the church, and our bodies as disciples, by which we continually experience the "fellowship of the Spirit."

The Spirit descends upon, dwells in, and (trans)forms real bodies. "God desires and loves and befriends human bodies. God the Spirit does not have disgust at the physical; she has *philia* for it; she takes up a place alongside (*para*) and in solidarity with it; she loves and befriends it; at creation she hovered over and at the resurrection will consummate it. The resurrection is above all things paraphysical."[10]

This means that because the Spirit has befriended matter, very ordinary things can become sacraments or channels of God's love and grace: oil and water and bread and wine; the bodies of human beings as they are baptized; the laying on of hands and anointing with oil; the human voice in the singing of songs.

Human beings are not just (or even primarily) "thinkers with ideas"; we are first and foremost embodied creatures who love, desire, tremble, rejoice, bless, and receive blessing. We don't inhabit the world mainly as cognitive machines. "Music, laughter, grief, and imagination keep breaking in despite the best efforts of the left brain."[11] In actual practice, we are creatures who love before we "see," who pray before we believe, who worship before we "know." We get fundamentally oriented to the world as living, breathing bodies enmeshed in a social context, a living tradition.[12]

Bodies matter in our formation. Formation in Christ through the Spirit is inescapably physical and bodily, not just intellectual and mystical.

The Way of Incarnation

Scripture portrays the Spirit as working through particular means and agents. Christ's disciples experience the Spirit, not as the first disciples experienced Jesus, but through the bodies of others, the life of the community, engagement with Scripture and other disciplines, and the sacramental practices of the church.

The Spirit forms us mostly through the use of "means." John Wesley spoke of "instituted means" and "prudential means." Instituted means include prayer, Bible study and meditation, the Lord's Supper, and Christian fellowship (reflecting the four practices of Acts 2:42–47). Prudential means include practices like small group meetings, using particular "rules" for personal growth, denying useless or tempting pleasures, watching against habitual sins, taking up one's cross, and "exercise of the presence of God."

Here I look briefly at four of the "means" of our formation by the Spirit.

The Community of Faith

When Paul envisions Christian life, he envisions communities, not primarily individuals. He doesn't lose the individual, but he thinks of individuals-in-community. For Paul, to be a Christian is to be a brother or sister in a new family, a citizen of a new polis, a vital organ in a new body. In our parlance we might say that being a Christian is a team sport.

Most of Paul's exhortations and directives involve communal practices and relationships with brothers and sisters—exemplified by the long list of "one anothers" scattered throughout his letters. Indeed, so strong is this focus that "we can say quite confidently that Paul would have almost nothing to say about the Christian life if he had to speak of it apart from the church." So when Paul speaks about the "Spirit-filled life," for example in Galatians 5:16–26 and Ephesians 5:18–21, he is not primarily addressing individuals but communities of faith. "Paul does not ponder salvation as the order of benefits applied to each individual by God. He envisions salvation as a reality that believers inhabit as bound-together communities that God animates and sustains by the Spirit." It may not be too far a stretch to say that for Paul the Spirit "eradicates the alleged border between individual and community."[13]

The Spirit forms and transforms us through "intimate relationships created by the Spirit with God (*Abba*), Jesus, and fellow believers."[14] For Paul, the Spirit's work is especially focused when believers are together. There, as a "fellowship of the Spirit," they experience the love of God and the grace of the Lord Jesus (2 Cor. 13:14). Paul expects Christians to have a radical commitment to one another, to care for and bear with one another, to bear burdens and be kind and compassionate to one another; indeed, to consider one another better than oneself. It is the presence of the Spirit in the body that enables all this "one-anotherness" to take place.

Christian formation, by the Spirit, is crippled when cut off from the community of faith, the body of Christ.

Scripture

If life in Christ takes place fundamentally in Spirit-filled community, then at its heart the church is a Scripture-reading community. The Spirit of God works powerfully through the proclaimed and written word of Scripture— to reveal Jesus, to release the life-transforming power of the gospel, to convict of sin, to renew our minds, to dynamically order the church, to situate us as saints in God's long story, to enlarge and refresh our grasp of God's mission in the world. As the writer of Hebrews notes, "For the word of God is living and active. Sharper than any double-edged sword, it penetrates even to dividing soul and spirit, joints and marrow; it judges the thoughts and attitudes of the heart" (Heb. 4:12). Christians also wield "the sword of the Spirit, which is the word of God" (Eph. 6:17).

Scripture, then, is both the product and the medium of the Spirit's work of new creation. The New Testament emerged as the written form of the powerful word that had broken into the lives of the first Christians and brought them tastes of life in its fullness. That written word, building upon and gradually placed alongside the old Scriptures of Israel, became the Spirit-empowered means by which Jesus' victory over the powers is being put into effect and by which life and order comes to the church. So the New Testament became the "new covenant charter, . . . the new telling of the story through which Christians are formed, reformed, and transformed so as to be God's people for God's world."[15] The Bible reveals a new world, one that reshapes our view of reality, a world where God's word powerfully encounters and transforms us.

Well-known Christian leader David Watson, as he was dying of cancer, captured the crucial role of Scripture in our lives: "God's word to us, especially his word spoken by his Spirit through the Bible, is the very ingredient that feeds our faith. If we feed our souls regularly on God's word, several times each day, we should become robust spiritually just as we feed on ordinary food several times each day, and become robust physically. Nothing is more important than hearing and obeying the word of God."[16]

This hearing of the word of God is no mere intellectual exercise. For not only did the Spirit of God move in and through those who first spoke and wrote this word; the Spirit continues to quicken this word, making it "living and active." The Scriptures are not simply information about the coming of God's kingdom and its final fulfillment; Scripture is a key part of the means by which the mission of God gets accomplished. Holy Scripture is itself a vehicle of the Spirit's ongoing mission to complete God's purposes for the creation.

Suffering and Trials

Suffering has been a normal experience for God's people in the Bible and ever since. Scripture makes it clear that the causes of suffering are varied. Sometimes it is due to the fallen creation that remains in travail. Sometimes it is the sin of others, and frequently it is our own doing or neglect. Sometimes we may experience suffering as God's discipline. Whatever the cause, around the globe and throughout history, the people of God suffer.

Paul makes an explicit connection between the role of suffering and the working of the Spirit in shaping us: "Not only so, but we also glory in our sufferings, because we know that suffering produces perseverance; perseverance, character; and character, hope. And hope does not put us to shame, because God's love has been poured out into our hearts through the Holy Spirit, who has been given to us" (Rom. 5:3–5). For the apostle, suffering is connected to our character formation in the Spirit-empowered community of faith—a shocking and unnerving insight.

James makes a similar point: "Consider it pure joy, my brothers, whenever you face trials of many kinds, because you know that the testing of your faith produces perseverance. Let perseverance finish its work so that you may be mature, and complete not lacking anything" (James 1:2–4; cf. 2 Pet 1:5–8). Suffering and testing are important means of our formation.

When suffering, oppression, and testing comes, how can we respond so that they become an intentional part of our formation? Suffering and trials open up new spaces in our lives, forcing our backs against the wall, and sometimes bringing us to the end of ourselves. These experiences can put us in a posture of welcoming God's discipline and grace.

We see a close connection, both in the New Testament and in our world today, between the Holy Spirit and the suffering, the poor, and the dispossessed. Jesus declared that the Spirit was upon him to declare good news to the oppressed and deliverance to the captives—the sufferers. They flocked to him. And today, in the Global South, it is the poor, the lowly, and the suffering who, by the millions, are finding in the outpouring of the Spirit new life and joy.

Suffering, sickness, and various forms of oppression bring home to us the truth that our formation in Christ is a formation in and as physical bodies. "Sickness makes it impossible to avoid the reality of our bodies. When I am sick, I am not a mind with a suffering body; I am the suffering body."[17] Our bodies matter; indeed, they are the very place in which the transforming of our lives into the image of Christ takes place. Life in the Spirit—our spiritual life—is not separated from life in our body. As persons we *are* our bodies—spirited bodies. It is our bodies that will be raised with Christ and transformed (Rom. 15).

Spiritual Disciplines

Formation by the Spirit is not at odds with exertion, practice, disciplines, and the formation of habits. These are necessary means. Grace is not opposed to effort, Dallas Willard was fond of saying, only to earning God's acceptance. The practices of the Christian faith, as one makes them part of one's spiritual growth plan, become "habitations of the Spirit."[18] The many different classic Christian disciplines become not means of lifting oneself up, but rather conduits or means of the Spirit's power and grace. I will look briefly at two approaches recommended by two influential writers: Dallas Willard and N. T. Wright.

Dallas Willard speaks of the "golden triangle" of spiritual growth. He places the *action of the Holy Spirit* at the top of the triangle, to indicate its central role in the whole process; at the bottom are the *ordinary events (or trials) of life* and the *chosen disciplines* for "putting on" a new heart.[19] Formation in the way of Christ happens in the steady interaction of these factors and forces. The Holy Spirit's work is crucial, but passive reliance on the Spirit will not transform our habits and thus our character. We must intentionally practice the way of Jesus. Willard stresses that "the training required to transform our most basic habits of thought, feeling, and action will not be done for us. And yet it is not something that we can do by ourselves."[20] God is at work within us, so we are to work out our salvation with fear and trembling (Phil. 2:12–13).

Willard points out that all of the spiritual disciplines involve the human body. That is the place where our deep habits reside and the place where new habits must be formed. So we cultivate the Christ-reflecting life by "directing our bodies into activities that empower the inner and outer person for God and through God." These activities are modeled after the activities of Jesus himself: they include solitude and silence, prayer, Scripture study and meditation, and service to others. Willard groups them into disciplines of abstinence (solitude and silence) and disciplines of engagement (study and worship). Practicing these disciplines is part of what Paul spoke of as offering our bodies as "living sacrifices" (Rom. 12:1).

These basic practices, Willard urges, should form the framework for a definite plan of action. In the Christian tradition, such a plan has been called a "rule of life." Such a rule is shaped for one's season of life, with its particular temptations, trials, and desired growth in Christ. This rule then becomes a kind of liturgy—repeated practices through which the Spirit works to form us in deep ways. What gets underplayed in Willard's vision is the church and its worship as the central place where this formation occurs.

N. T. Wright likes to picture the path to Christian maturity and holiness as a circle of five basic practices in the community of faith—what he calls the "virtuous circle."[21] They include Scripture, stories, examples, community, and practices. All of them take place in the atmosphere or environment of the Spirit's presence and enabling power. One can break into the circle at any one of the five elements.

Scripture is the basic element and natural starting point. By steadily immersing ourselves in its reading—and its singing—we gradually begin to locate ourselves as actors in God's long and ongoing drama. *Stories*, primarily in Scripture but stories of all kinds, open up to us what it means to be human, reveal the importance of love and beauty, deepen our capacities for compassion, and grow in us wisdom and discernment. *Examples* are exemplary persons, like the dozen examples of faith in Hebrews 11, who show us aspects of the life of faithfulness and virtue—and these examples extend to the saints throughout Christian history, from a Perpetua (martyred in the early third century) to a Francis of Assisi (in the thirteenth) to a Dietrich Bonhoeffer (in the twentieth). *Community* provides the context for the formation of the habits of the Christian heart and life—these are local, often small communities where friendship and the fruit of the Spirit are being learned and practiced. Finally, to complete the circle, regular *practices* constantly orient the people of God to their mission—the central practice is worship, centered around the Word, the Lord's Supper, and baptism.

The practice of reading and teaching Scripture holds all these elements together. Scripture, as Wright says, is habit-forming and thus character-forming. To have Christ formed in us, through the Spirit, is to learn the habits of the Christian heart and life. Through steady practices, individually but mostly in Christian community, we acquire "the second-nature habits of self-giving love."[22] The Spirit is at work through these habit-forming practices so that the character traits or virtues that result can be said to be Spirit-formed.

Stanley Hauerwas asserts that a key dimension of being Christian is "to have one's body shaped, one's habits determined, in such a manner that the worship of God is unavoidable." Such a statement sounds strange to us who revel in and demand our individual freedoms and preferences. The claim here is that holiness is not primarily a matter of private creation, but "the result of our being made part of a body that makes it impossible for us to be anything other than disciples."[23] That is to say, in the body of

Christ, which is the sphere of the Spirit's power, we get trained—or, rather, habituated—in the ways of Jesus, so that what is in the beginning strange and unnatural to us becomes normal, even natural. In the body of Christ— if indeed the Spirit is welcomed and not quenched—we get formed into disciples who cannot help but be disciples.

I turn now to focus on how the Spirit forms believers through worship, the centering event of life in God's kingdom.

Formative Liturgies

Let's begin with the concept of a liturgy. James Smith argues that human beings are fundamentally "liturgical animals"—that is, our orientation to the world is governed more by what we love than what we think—and that our loves are shaped by the rituals or liturgies that, consciously or unconsciously, we adopt. These liturgies can be sacred or secular, religious or cultural. So there is the liturgy of the American shopping mall that forms us, through its embodied practices and rituals, into consumers. And there is the liturgy of the sports stadium that forms us into devoted fans.[24] Liturgies are sets of habitual practices that instill in our hearts, through our bodies, visions of the good life. They form our very identities by shaping our most fundamental desires or loves. They are love-shaping practices. Liturgies can do this because we are the sorts of creatures "whose orientation to the world is shaped from the body up more than from the head down."[25]

Liturgies form in us what we are most devoted to, what we most desire. They calibrate our hearts. We are all being formed powerfully—into consumers, into passionate sports fans, maybe into Christian disciples—by sets of ritual practices that may be mostly unconscious to us. They often shape our imaginations and our desires before we have even thought much about them.

From a Christian perspective, these cultural liturgies easily and regularly deform us—that is, recruit our loves toward other gods, other ultimate ends. So the liturgy of Christian worship becomes the recalibration station for our hearts, for the reordering of our desires toward God. In worship we experience "de-idolizing."[26] There we see with new clarity the forces and institutions by which we form God in our own image and after our own desires. For in worship we encounter—with our bodies, hearts, and minds—the God of life, confessing the lordship of Jesus and opening our lives to the Spirit's transformation. Week by week in the liturgy of Christian worship, we get reoriented by the story of God and God's people, and our habits and deep reflexes get reshaped by the Spirit, re-forming our character so that we can live into God's vision for the reconciliation and renewal of all things (Col. 1:20).

To be clear, "liturgy" refers not just to the style of worship often called "liturgical" or "high church," but rather more broadly to the "formative, embodied practices" that make up Christian worship across a range of styles and traditions. The basic practices of historic Christian worship provide steady channels for the Spirit's work of forming us into a people able and willing to follow Jesus Christ in his way of loving and serving the world. In worship, one could say, we rehearse those practices, allowing our bodies and hearts to form new habits, new reflexes.

We can affirm, with James Smith, that "[t]he church's worship is a uniquely intense site of the Spirit's transformative presence." It is a "hot spot" where we encounter the living God. A feature of Christian worship, unparalleled in other religions, was (and is) the presence of the living Lord in the midst of his assembled people (Matt. 18:20; 28:20). In our worship, the Spirit of Christ continues the presence of Christ, bringing the love of Christ, making alive the words of Christ, and giving the gifts of Christ. We "worship in the Spirit of God and boast in Christ Jesus" (Phil 3:3 NRSV). And in our encounter with this presence, we should be clear that our formation is not the *point* of worship but rather a by-product of our praise of and communion with the Trinity.[27]

Let's also be clear that "spiritual" worship in the New Testament never excluded or minimized the body and the physical. We didn't get our suspicion of embodied worship from Scripture. Early Christian worship involved robust singing in the Spirit, holy kisses, anointing with oil, washing of feet, gathering around a table, drinking wine and eating bread, bowing and kneeling, raising one's hands, preaching, and praying aloud. "To engage in worship requires a body," Smith notes, "with lungs to sing, knees to kneel, legs to stand, arms to raise, eyes to weep, noses to smell, tongues to taste, ears to hear, hands to hold and raise. Christian worship is not the sort of thing that ethereal, disembodied spirits could engage in."[28]

Worship Requires a Body

Let's look briefly at seven basic liturgical practices that emerged out of Scripture and the worship of the early church: gathering, praying, singing, confessing the faith, hearing the word, baptizing and communing, and sending.

Gathering

The people of God are a gathered people, called out from every tribe, nation, and tongue to be a new nation, a peculiar people. The "call to worship" gathers this new people in its local setting. That in fact is what the word church (*ekklesia*) means: the called-out assembly. We are called out and assembled to be constituted into the end-time community. Yet in our own typically "tribal" gatherings, it becomes clear that we fall quite short of that end-time communion of saints—that "great multitude . . . from every nation, tribe, people and language, standing before the throne and before the Lamb" (Rev. 7:9). We are still a broken and fractured assembly, where some are not welcome or find insurmountable barriers to belonging.

But on the Lord's Day we are called to assemble as a part of that "great multitude," to declare, in advance of the reality, that we are joining with the one people of God. And the worship leader issues a call to worship, often from the Psalms:

> Come, let us bow down in worship,
> Let us kneel before the LORD our Maker,
> for he is our God
>> and we are the people of his pasture,
>> the flock under his care. (Ps. 95:6–7)

We are being invited to assemble "in the Spirit," in the transforming presence of God, where we are raised up to sit in heavenly places with the

Father and the Son (Eph. 2:6). In this assembly to which we are called, the Spirit of Christ meets us and mediates among us the riches of Christ, opening us up to the great and wonderful end-time assembly around God's throne (Heb. 12:22–24; Rev 7:9–15).[29]

Praying

Prayer is a key means by which the Spirit works to bring in God's kingdom. Luke pictures the earliest Christian community as devoted to prayer. The earliest disciples in the upper room after Jesus' ascension "all joined together constantly in prayer" (Acts 1:14). Facing opposition from Jewish leaders, "they raised their voices together in prayer to God" (4:24). "After they prayed, . . . they were all filled with the Holy Spirit and spoke the word of God boldly" (4:31). Paul also exhorts the churches he planted to be devoted to prayer (Rom. 12:12; Col 4:2), and to "pray in the Spirit on all occasions with all kinds of prayers" (Eph. 6:18).

In public prayer in the worship assembly, we assume and declare a different view of how the world works—different from secular assumptions about the conduct of life. We declare that God attends to us, draws us into relationship with the Trinity, and cares about the concrete things that human beings face. So in worship, because Jesus has opened the way to the Father for us, we respond to the scriptural admonition: "Let us then approach the throne of grace with confidence, so that we may receive mercy and find grace to help in our time of need" (Heb. 4:16).

In the assembly we pray prayers of intercession and for illumination. In intercessory prayer, because we are called to be God's ambassadors to our neighborhoods and the world, we pray for the poor and the prisoners, for the suffering and the persecuted, for healing from illness, for protection from abuse, for the eradication of racism and war—for the brokenness of creation. For this reason, intercessory prayer will often be marked by lament—the cry for the coming of "new creation." Prayer for illumination, usually connected to the preaching of the Word, is the prayer for our hearts to be opened, our minds made receptive, so that we can receive God's truth. It is a prayer for the Spirit to enable our understanding, since we have received "the Spirit who is from God, so that we may understand what God has freely given us" (1 Cor. 2:12). With such prayer we are trained in the habit of receptivity to and dependence on God.

Singing

Throughout all of Scripture, singing is deeply connected to the worship of God. The Psalms, many of which were intended for use in congregational worship in the temple, connect divine presence and singing in various ways. We come into God's presence with songs (Ps. 95:2; 100:2). In times of trial God immerses us in songs: "you will protect me from trouble and surround me with songs of deliverance" (Ps. 32:7). Singing expressed the sometimes overwhelming joy of life with Yahweh: "My lips will shout for joy when I sing praises to you; my soul also, which you have rescued" (Ps. 71:23). The book of Psalms is one long invitation to see and experience the dynamic presence of the Almighty among the people of God.

Paul relates singing in worship to the filling of the Holy Spirit. The Spirit's presence stirs new songs in God's worshippers and fills their hearts with singing (Eph. 5:18–19). Indeed, singing itself appears to be a means by which we are filled with the Spirit and through which the word of Christ dwells in us richly (Col. 3:16).

Singing involves a kind of full-bodied engagement in worship, engaging vocal chords, lungs, tongues, minds, and emotions, and easily drawing our whole bodies into movement. And because of this, singing opens a path into our hearts and imaginations. Songs get absorbed into the very core of our lives, and because of that, singing has a singular power to shape us in deep ways.

Singing in worship has the power to take us beyond ourselves, awakening us to the splendor, majesty, power, and truth of God. George Herbert, England's greatest devotional poet, called church music "the way to heaven's door."[30] Singing enables us to experience and enjoy God's presence, not simply to think about it. It also draws us into the worshipping community, making us attentive to others, not just our own solitude and feelings.

Basil the Great, fourth-century theologian of the Spirit, spoke of how the Spirit "charms" us into embracing God's truth: "The Holy Spirit sees how much difficulty mankind has in loving virtue, and how we prefer the lure of pleasure to the straight and narrow path. What does he do? He adds the grace of music to the truth of doctrine. Charmed by what we hear, we pluck the fruit of the words without realizing it."[31] Other writers in the ancient Christian tradition spoke of "singing in jubilation" as a normal way of letting the Spirit pray within one. For Augustine in the early fifth century, "this kind of singing is a sound which means that the heart is giving birth to something it cannot speak of."[32]

Congregational singing is a central formative practice of worship. This practice is under pressure in our time, as worshippers easily become mostly an audience for the singing of gifted professionals.

Confessing the Faith

Confession of faith quickly became a basic practice in early worship assemblies. We see such confessions in Scripture:

> Great indeed, we confess, is the mystery of our religion:
> > He appeared in a body,
> > was vindicated by the Spirit,
> > was seen by angels,
> > was preached among the nations,
> > was believed on in the world,
> > was taken up in glory. (1 Tim. 3:16)

Another creedal passage is 1 Corinthians 15:3–5, where Paul says he is transmitting to the Corinthian church what he received as a sacred tradition: "For what I received I passed on to you as of first importance: that Christ died for our sins according to the Scriptures, that he was buried, that he was raised on the third day according to the Scriptures, and that he appeared to Cephas, and then to the Twelve."

From its early days, the church's worship included a confession of faith. The early Christians developed "rules of faith" summarizing "the Apostles' teaching" (Acts 2:42); these short summaries were recited by candidates for baptism and in the worship gatherings. The Apostles Creed was one of these early rules of faith, and in the succeeding centuries has been perhaps the most universal Christian confession. (You can read it in the Resources section of this book.)

When we confess our faith in worship, using the Apostles' Creed or some other orthodox summary of the faith, we engage in a powerful formative practice. We can call it the Christian's "pledge of allegiance." We are declaring our allegiance to another kingdom, to another Lord (not Caesar, not the president or prime minister), to another story of what is real and true (not the story of modern autonomy and individualism), and to a different way of being in the world (the way of sacrifice, joy, dependency, and peaceableness).

According to John Webster, confessing our faith involves "a denial of untruth and a glad and courageous affirmation of truth." It is "to take sides, to pledge involvement with a particular cause, by binding oneself to a particular reading of reality."[33] Such confession, in a culture of individual autonomy where truth is mostly private and personal, is deeply countercultural and deeply formative. It is deeply puzzling to me why so many churches of our time seldom if ever make confession of the faith part of their liturgy.

Hearing the Word

Scripture provides the overarching narrative that most fundamentally shapes the identity of the people of God. It a rich and complex story, and the learning of that story and the living into that story in the regular rhythms of the church's life fundamentally shape the kind of people Christians are called to be. Over time we come to understand ourselves as characters within God's ongoing story.

The reading and proclamation of Scripture stand as a centerpiece of Christian worship. It is a key means by which the Spirit shapes our lives toward the image of Jesus and the large purposes of God. The reading of Scripture in worship is not simply the imparting of new or forgotten information. It probably does that too, and there is an important place for serious teaching of the faith. But in the liturgy of worship, the reading of Scripture is a central aspect of the praise of God; in reading portions of the biblical story, we are rehearsing the mighty deeds of God through Israel's history, through Jesus Christ, and through the pouring out of the Spirit. We are celebrating, praising, and worshipping God. It is a way of acclaiming God's love and might that is just as important—even more so—than singing wonderful worship songs.

In so-called "high church" worship services that follow the classic lectionary, there are normally four major Scripture readings: from the Old Testament, the Psalms, the Gospels, and the Epistles. In many "low church" and charismatic worship services, there may be only one Scripture reading, usually associated with the sermon—or none except short quotes in the sermon. In many of these churches, Scripture reading in public worship has become thin, even perfunctory. If Scripture is "living and active," providing the grand story by which our desires and our aspirations are shaped, and if its reading in worship is a way of praising God, then it seems strange to me that "Bible-believing" churches don't make its reading prominent in their liturgies.

The renewal of Scripture reading in worship can happen in different ways, reflecting different worship styles and traditions. Using the lectionary is one good way. Whatever the plan, churches should engage the whole scope of the Bible's story. One guideline is to have at least two readings—one from the Old Testament and one from the New. This is a way of reminding us week in and week out that Scripture tells an overarching story, one that we are called to live into—that we are not just hearing a piece of wisdom here and some useful advice there. An important role of the sermon then becomes making connections and situating specific texts within the sweep of God's big story. In this way, through the steady reading and proclaiming of this story, the people of God are "renewed in knowledge in the image of the creator" (Col. 3:10).

Baptizing and Communing

The Nicene Creed confesses "one baptism for the forgiveness of sins." Baptism demonstrates and proclaims that, though death hangs over this present age, death has been defeated by the victory of Christ and that through the Spirit we enter into the life of the age to come.

Baptism is a Spirit event—"in one Spirit we were all baptized into one body" (1 Cor. 12:13, ESV)—and it announces and enacts a new social reality, a new community or polis. That is why baptism is situated in the context of the church's worship. It is not just a private transaction between an individual and God. It is rather an initiation into the people of God, who live by a different story and form a different kind of community. In baptism the privileges of social class, pedigree, and worldly status and the boundaries of tribe and ethnic identity get overturned—all in favor of a "peculiar people": "all of you who were baptized into Christ have clothed yourselves with Christ. There is neither Jew nor Gentile, neither slave nor free, nor is there male and female, for you are all one in Christ Jesus" (Gal. 3:27–28).

In baptism we receive a new identity, a new orientation to the world. Baptism symbolizes—and helps enact—the obliteration of old distinctions, old habits, old racial and economic barriers. Through baptism one enters a community of equals where people learn to give up hope in themselves and the old securities.

A baptismal prayer in the classic liturgy says: "We thank you, Father, for the water of baptism. In it we are buried with Christ in his death. By it we share in his resurrection. Through it we are reborn by the Holy Spirit. Therefore in joyful obedience to your Son, we bring into his fellowship those who come to him in faith, baptizing them in the name of the Father, of the Son, and of the Holy Spirit."[34]

The Lord's Supper, also situated in the midst of gathered worship, is the feast of forgiveness and reconciliation. It is a celebration of God's forgiveness of those who were once God's enemies, but also a communion with one another—which calls for facing up to the reality of strained and fractured relationships. It is not a devotional exercise for private, isolated individuals, but rather a time for experiencing the "fellowship of the Holy Spirit" in concrete ways.

Both Jesus and Paul admonished disciples to examine themselves and seek reconciliation before bringing one's gift or partaking of the Lord's Supper (Matt. 5:23–24; 1 Cor. 11:27–34). Paul is distressed at the Corinthians' disregard for one another in the presence of Christ at the Lord's table. They have not discerned Christ's presence; they have not submitted themselves to one another (1 Cor. 11). Like baptism, communion was meant to enact and foster a new social reality. It was meant to train us in submitting to one another, in practicing reconciliation with one another, and in learning how to welcome one another, however separated we may have been.

"Hounded constantly by the world's vision of success and power, we are confronted, around Christ's table, with a contrary vision—the way of weakness and the power of reconciling love. Week by week that vision takes hold of us. Week by week, as we gather around the table, we are fashioned by God into a cruciform people. There we gradually find ourselves open to ways of living in this world that we had not considered possible."[35]

Sending

In worship we are engaging with God through the Spirit, and in that engagement being trained to engage in the mission of God, to take up our vocation as God's image bearers. So at the end of the gathering, we are sent from the "practice arena" into the wider world to be witnesses of the Crucified One and agents of God's "new creation." We are sent out to live out of and to tell a different story. We are sent out to make disciples, telling good news of Christ, the New Human, and demonstrating what redeemed human community looks like. So we are affirmed as God's beloved, commissioned for his mission, and blessed as God's children:

> The LORD bless you and keep you;
> The LORD make his face shine on you
> and be gracious to you;
> The LORD turn his face toward you
> and give you peace. (Num. 6:24–26)

Formation for Mission

If the way of Christ gets habituated in our bodies so that the practices of life in the kingdom shape our life patterns and relationships, then perhaps we can picture the Holy Spirit as an artist. The Spirit is transforming believers into the likeness of the risen Christ with "ever-increasing glory" (2 Cor. 3:18). So picture the Spirit as a painter of pictures.

The artist's palette holds a wonderful array of colors. But the Spirit's one subject is Christ. The Spirit seeks "to paint countless portraits of that subject on countless human canvases using the paints and brushes provided by countless human cultures and historical situations." So the Spirit "takes the human material that makes you you and me me and, in a way that is authentic to what God made each of us to be. . . , sets us free from our fallenness and begins to sanctify and transform us into yet another portrait of Christ."[36]

When through Christ the Spirit is given to us, two things follow: on the one hand, the Spirit draws us into deeper oneness with Christ and with his Body; on the other, the Spirit accentuates what is distinctive and specific to us as individual persons. In the biblical story, people are made to grow, and the Spirit fosters growth in the powers and capacities particular to each of us.

But the path of formation centered in the Triune God—intimacy with Christ through the Spirit and sharing in God's mission—is not simply a search for personal meaning and inner peace. The Bible is not a manual for a privatized escapist spirituality. "The great weakness of North American spirituality is that it is all about us: fulfilling our potential, getting in on the blessings of God, expanding our influence, finding our gifts, getting a handle on principles by which we can get an edge on the competition."[37]

Christian formation easily becomes turned inward and narcissistic. As followers of the crucified and risen Messiah, we want and require deep formation, but we want it to be oriented toward God's mission. We want formation for mission.

Our formative disciplines, our "rules of life," and our worship liturgies should continually orient us outward, centering us in Christ and through the Spirit moving us out into the mission of God. Our worship—the prayers, confession of faith, preaching, and songs—can orient us inward to ourselves, to our own needs and consolations, or it can steadily orient us outward to the unbelieving world; it can maintain an introverted congregation focusing mainly on practices of maintenance, or it can steadily orient members toward the horizon of Jesus' mission.

So we ask questions. Is the focus on individual enjoyment and renewal or on living out empowered lives for the sake of the world? Are we following the risen Christ in the call to give up our lives or mainly meeting our therapeutic needs?

What does the life formed in Christ through the Spirit look like? It looks like this:

> You must be tender-hearted, kind, humble, meek, and ready
> to put up with anything. You must bear with one another and,
> if anyone has a complaint against someone else, you must
> forgive each other. . . . On top of all this you must put on love,
> which ties everything together and makes it complete. . . . And
> whatever you do, in word or action, do everything in the name
> of the master, Jesus, giving thanks through him to God the
> father. (Col. 3:12–14, 17 KNT)

And this:

> [If there is] any common sharing in the Spirit, if any tenderness
> and compassion, then make my joy complete by being like-
> minded, having the same love, being one in spirit and of one
> mind. Do nothing out of selfish ambition or vain conceit. Rather,
> in humility value others above yourselves, not looking to your
> own interests but each of you to the interests of the others.
> (Phil 2:1–4 KNT)

And also this: "You are all children of light, children of the day! We don't belong to the night, or to darkness. So, then, let's not go to sleep like the others, but let's stay awake and remain in control of ourselves" (1 Thess. 5:6–11 KNT). In the death and resurrection of the Messiah, the new day has already dawned. God's reign, God's future, is breaking in. A renewed humanity is being formed, patterned after Jesus, the New Human. A new way of living is called for—and now made possible through the Spirit of Jesus. Christian formation is about forming "the habits of the daytime heart in a world still full of darkness."[38]

The very dynamic of formation in Christ points beyond the self, in two directions: to God in worship, and to the world in mission. We can say that life in Christ is lived in the steady rhythm of worship and witness or mission.

Notice how the call to holiness—which is the goal of formation—is a call to step into the long trajectory of the mission of God for his people to be "a light to the nations." Paul again: "Do everything without grumbling or arguing, so that you may become blameless and pure, 'children of God without fault in a warped and crooked generation.' Then you will shine like lights in the world as you hold firmly to the word of life" (Phil 2:14–16 KNT). This is what the prophet Isaiah had envisioned for the age to come: "Arise, shine, for your light has come, and the glory of the LORD rises upon you" (Isa. 60:1). This call is being realized among those who by the Spirit proclaim Jesus as Lord and thus reveal "the glory of God the Father" (Phil. 2:11).

The call to holiness for the sake of God's mission means that disciples must "put off your former lifestyle, the old humanity. . . . and you must put on the new humanity, which is being created the way God intended it, displaying justice and genuine holiness" (Eph. 4:22, 24 KNT). Becoming a people who "display" justice and holiness involves "putting off" and "putting on." As we have seen, formation by the Spirit is not at odds with exertion, practice, disciplines, and the formation of habits. Indeed, these are the normal means of the Spirit's work in us. "Liturgy is the way we learn to 'put on' Christ (Col. 3:12–16)."[39]

The mission of God, as we will see more fully in Chapter Eight, is cruciform. The energy, the dynamic power, of God's kingdom is self-giving love. It is the work of the Spirit to pour this love—the love shared among the Trinity—into our lives, as we are willing and able to receive it. The presence of this kind of love is a sign of the end time breaking into the present. To become agents and emissaries of that kingdom is to be steadily and intentionally formed with the habits and character traits of that self-giving way.

NOTES

[1] Jeffrey Greenman, *Life in the Spirit: Spiritual Formation in Theological Perspective*, ed. Jeffrey Greenman and George Kalantzis (Downers Grove, IL: IVP Academic, 2010), 24.

[2] Charles Taylor, *A Secular Age* (Cambridge, MA: Harvard University, 2007), 746.

[3] Taylor, *A Secular Age*, 548.

[4] C. S. Lewis, *Mere Christianity*, (1952; New York: HarperCollins, 2001), Bk 2, chap 5, 64.

[5] Colin Gunton, *The Christian Faith: An Introduction to Christian Doctrine* (Oxford: Blackwell, 2002), 9.

[6] Nancey Murphey, *Bodies and Souls, or Spirited Bodies?* (Cambridge, UK: Cambridge University, 2006), ix.

[7] Jürgen Moltmann, *The Spirit of Life: A Universal Affirmation*, trans. Margaret Kohl (Minneapolis: Fortress, 1992), 95.

[8] N. T. Wright, *The Resurrection of the Son of God* (Minneapolis: Fortress, 2003), 347–56.

[9] Eugene Rogers, *After the Spirit: A Constructive Pneumatology from Resources outside the Modern West* (Grand Rapids: Eerdmans, 2005), 58.

[10] Rogers, *After the Spirit*, 103–04.

[11] N. T. Wright, *Surprised by Scripture: Engaging Contemporary Issues* (New York: HarperCollins, 2014), 139.

[12] For more on these themes, see James K. A. Smith, *Desiring the Kingdom: Worship, Worldview, and Cultural Formation* (Grand Rapids: Baker Academic, 2009).

[13] Timothy Gombis, "Participation in the New-Creation People of God in Christ by the Spirit," in *The Apostle Paul and the Christian Life*, ed. Scot McKnight and Joseph Modica (Grand Rapids: Baker Academic, 2016), 112, 115; John R. Levison, *Filled with the Spirit* (Grand Rapids: Eerdmans, 2009), 306.

[14] Volker Rabens, *The Holy Spirit and Ethics in Paul: Transformation and Empowering for Religious-Ethical Life* (Minneapolis: Fortress, 2013), 126.

[15] N. T. Wright, *The Last Word: Scripture and the Authority of God* (San Francisco: HarperSanFrancisco, 2005), 59. As Telford Work puts it, "the Bible is now the Church's own heritage, horizon, formation, practice, authority, instrument, medium, teaching, criterion, witness, confession, community, and glory." *Living and Active: Scripture in the Economy of Salvation* (Grand Rapids: Eerdmans, 2002), 216.

[16] David Watson, *Fear No Evil: A Personal Struggle with Cancer* (London, 1984), quoted by Dallas Willard, *The Spirit of the Disciplines: Understanding How God Changes* (New York: HarperCollins, 1988), 176–77.

[17] Stanley Hauerwas, "The Sanctified Body," in *Embodied Holiness: Toward a Corporate Theology of Spiritual Growth*, ed. Samuel Powell and Michael Lodahl (Downers Grove, IL: InterVarsity, 1999), 29.

[18] Craig Dykstra, *Growing in the Life of Faith* (Philadelphia: Westminster John Knox, 2005), 63.

[19] Dallas Willard, *The Divine Conspiracy: Rediscovering Our Hidden Life in God* (San Francisco: HarperSanFrancisco, 1998), 347–64.

[20] Willard, *Divine Conspiracy*, 345–46.

[21] N. T. Wright, *After You Believe: Why Christian Character Matters* (New York: HarperCollins, 2010), 259–84.

[22] Wright, *After You Believe*, 264, 270.

[23] Hauerwas, "The Sanctified Body," 22, 28.

[24] "As is well-known, Friday night high school football is the most significant liturgical event in Texas." Stanley Hauerwas, *In Good Company* (Notre Dame, IN: University of Notre Dame Press, 1995), chapter 10.

[25] Smith, *Desiring the Kingdom*, 25. See also his *You Are What You Love: The Spiritual Power of Habit* (Grand Rapids: Brazos, 2016).

[26] Gerhard Lohfink, *Does God Need the Church?: Toward a Theology of the People of God* (Collegeville, MN: Liturgical Press, 1999), 217.

[27] Smith, *Desiring the Kingdom*, 150.

[28] Smith, *Desiring the Kingdom*, 139.

[29] See John Mark Hicks, Johnny Melton, and Bobby Valentine, *A Gathered People: Revisioning the Assembly as Transforming Encounter* (Abilene, TX: Leafwood, 2007), esp. 129–49.

[30] George Herbert, "Church Music," cited by Darryl Tippens, *Pilgrim Heart: The Way of Jesus in Everyday Life* (Abilene, TX: Leafwood, 2006), 147. Tippens, in an unusual move, includes singing in his treatment of basic Christian practices or disciplines that make up an "embodied spirituality" (145–55).

[31] Basil the Great, quoted by J. Gelineau, "Music and Singing in the Liturgy," in *The Study of Liturgy*, rev. edition (Oxford: Oxford University Press, 1997), 496.

[32] Augustine of Hippo, *Sermons on the Psalms* 32.8, cited by Sarah Coakley, *God, Sexuality, and the Self: An Essay "On the Trinity"* (Cambridge, UK: Cambridge University Press, 2013), 175.

[33] John Webster, "Confession and Confessions," in *Nicene Christianity: The Future of a New Ecumenism*, ed. Christopher Seitz (Grand Rapids: Brazos, 2001), 124, 125.

[34] *The Book of Common Prayer* (New York: Church Publishing, 2007), 306–7.

[35] Leonard Allen, *The Cruciform Church: Becoming a Cross-Shaped People in a Secular World*, anniversary edition (1990; Abilene, TX: Abilene Christian University, 2016), 153.

[36] Thomas Smail, *The Giving Gift: The Holy Spirit in Person* (London: Hodder, 1988), 77, 180.

[37] Eugene Peterson, *Christ Plays in Ten Thousand Places* (Grand Rapids: Eerdmans, 2005), 335.

[38] Wright, *After You Believe*, 137.

[39] Smith, *You Are What You Love*, 69.

7

SOARING

> Through the Spirit we become partakers of God's life,
> caught up into the joy and fullness of that life.

Those who hope in the LORD *will renew their strength.*
They will soar on wings like eagles; they will run and not grow weary,
they will walk and not be faint.
—Isaiah 40:31

We believe in the Holy Spirit, the Lord, the giver of life, . . .
With the Father and the Son he is worshiped and glorified.
—Nicene Creed (381)

If we are seized by the Spirit of the resurrection, we get up out of our
sadness and apathy. We begin to flower and become fruitful again.
—Jürgen Moltman

Lord is the title given to Jesus in the New Testament, and also the name used
in the Greek version of the Old Testament (LXX) to represent the Hebrew
name of God, Yahweh. The second article of the Nicene Creed says, "We
believe . . . in one Lord Jesus Christ, the only Son of God." In the third
article, the same lordship is assigned to the Holy Spirit. In addition, the
creed declares that through the Son "all things were made"; the third article
parallels this with the affirmation of the Spirit as "life-giver"—that is, the
Spirit as the one who fills with life what is made by the Son.

"Lord and Giver of Life"

The image of the Spirit as life-giver, of course, comes from the Gospel of John. "The Spirit gives life," says Jesus. "The words I have spoken to you—they are full of the Spirit and life" (John 6:63). An important scriptural image for the Spirit is the wellspring or water of life. To the Samaritan woman at the well, Jesus says, "Whoever drinks the water I give them will never thirst. Indeed, the water I give them will become in them a spring of water welling up to eternal life" (4:14). From this well flows water that restores and nourishes all that is withered and parched and dried up. Jesus invites anyone who is thirsty to believe in him, and "rivers of living water will flow from within him"—a reference to the Spirit whom believers were to receive (John 7:37–38).

Scripture contains no more vivid and dramatic image of God's Spirit as the giver of life than Ezekiel's vision of the valley of dry bones. Israel had experienced catastrophe and desolation with the annihilation of Jerusalem in 587 BC. In Babylonian exile they say, "Our bones are dried up and our hope is gone; we are cut off" (Ezek. 37:11).

Before this devastation, the prophet had observed the nation's descent stage by stage. He had seen a vision of the glory departing in stages from the temple, but could still envision Israel responding to the Lord's initiative; he had thought they could repent, put away their idols, and make a new heart for themselves (Ezek. 18:30–31). But after 587 BC, not a trace of hope is left. So devastating was the destruction and exile that Israel has no life left.

In this context of hopelessness and powerlessness, Ezekiel declares this oracle from the Lord: "I will give you a new heart, and a new spirit I will put within you, and I will remove the heart of stone from your flesh and give you a heart of flesh. And I will put my Spirit within you" (Ezek. 36:26–27 ESV). Israel has no life of its own left to make a new heart and a new spirit.

The Spirit transports the prophet to a valley of the dead where sun-bleached bones are scattered. The Lord, he says, "brought me out in the Spirit of the LORD and set me down in the middle of the valley; it was full of bones. And he led me around among them, and behold, there were very many on the surface of the valley, and behold, they were very dry" (Ezek.

37:1–2 ESV). God asks, "Son of man, can these bones live?" (37:3). Even the fertile imagination of Ezekiel cannot imagine life in this desolate valley: "Sovereign Lord, you alone know."

Then the Lord says to him, "Prophesy over these bones . . . . Thus says the Lord God to these bones: I will cause breath [spirit] to enter you, and you shall live. And I will lay sinews upon you, and cause flesh to come upon you, and cover you with skin, and put breath [spirit] in you, and you shall live" (37:4–6 ESV). The bones get reconnected and enfleshed. But there is still no breath or spirit.

So Ezekiel is told to "prophesy to the breath [spirit]. . . 'Come from the four winds, O breath, and breathe into these slain, that they may live'" (37:9 ESV). And say to them, "Behold, I will open your graves and raise you from your graves, O my people" (37:12 ESV). After these words, "breath came into them, and they lived and stood on their feet—an exceedingly great army" (37:10). There was "a grand rattle of re-creation, an astounding inbreathing of the spirit, and the formation of Israel anew."[1]

Through the Spirit, the multitude of people "stood on their feet." This had been Ezekiel's own experience, on two occasions, of filling with the Spirit. First was his prophetic call, where he describes an encounter with the glory of the Lord. "When I saw it," he says, "I fell facedown, and I heard the voice of one speaking. As he spoke, the Spirit came into me and raised me to my feet" (Ezek. 1:28–2:2). The second experience was similar: "And the glory of the LORD was standing there, like the glory I had seen by the Kebar River, and I fell facedown. Then the Spirit came into me and raised me to my feet" (Ezek. 3:23–24).

Both Ezekiel's own experience and his dramatic vision of the valley of death attest that the Spirit of God is the powerful giver of life. "I will put my Spirit within you, and *you shall live*" (Ezek. 37:14).

This story of the valley of the very dry bones provides an important backdrop for the way Paul envisions the giving of the Spirit to Christians.[2] Paul can summarize the rich experience of the Spirit in believers and in the fellowship of believers in one word: *life*. The Spirit is the giver of new life. "But if Christ is in you, then even though your body is subject to death because of sin, the Spirit gives life because of righteousness" (Rom. 8:10).

The Spirit of God is "life" because the Spirit transforms death into life: in the present the Spirit brings life *out of* brokenness and deadness in sin, and in the future the Spirit will bring life *beyond* physical death just as in the raising of Jesus (8:11).

Paul, unlike Ezekiel, is not envisioning the resurrection of a whole nation but a resurrection in more personal terms. But it is a "new creation" nonetheless—life out of hopelessness and death, and just as dramatic. When Paul faced enormous affliction, even feeling "the sentence of death," he relied on the "God who raises the dead" (2 Cor. 1:8–10) by the Spirit. And the Spirit's power in him has a Trinitarian shape: "It is *God* who makes both us and you stand firm in *Christ*. He anointed us, set his seal of ownership on us, and put his *Spirit* in our hearts as a deposit [or pledge]" (2 Cor. 1:21–22 italics added; cf. 1 Thess. 5:16–19). Levison summarizes that the Spirit is "given as a pledge that Ezekiel's magnificent vision of resurrection will flood the shadow of death, will replace outwardly decaying bodies with a jolt of spirit-filled life, with a lavish outpouring of vitality (2 Cor. 5:5)."[3]

Moltmann likes to speak of the Spirit as a "torrent of energy" and vitality. Flooded by the energy of the Spirit, "body and soul awaken like flowers in the spring and become fruitful—that is, they themselves become life that gives life." Experiencing this life, our bodies begin to radiate—in the "glowing face, the shining eyes, the speaking mouth, the play of features and the gestures which show affection and commitment." Experiencing this life, we begin to be conformed to Jesus' life with his "healing, radiating, and loving way of living," as well as to his struggle with the powers of destruction.[4] One day, through his Spirit, we expect to become "like in form to his glorious body" (Phil. 3:21).

The Spirit of life is not miserly, granting new life in meager little quantities. The Spirit is the abundant "living water," a strong and lavish outpouring like water gushing through a desert land (Isa. 43:20), like "a spring of water welling up to eternal life" (John 4:14). The Spirit of life is more rich and profuse than the best spring rains or overflowing rivers that soak the ground and make it fertile (Ezek. 47:1–12).

A twelfth-century Christian theologian and songwriter gave us this hymn about the life-giving Spirit:

> The Holy Spirit: living and life-giving,
> the life that's all things moving,
> the root in all created being:
> of filth and muck it washes all things clean—
> out-scrubbing guilty staining, its balm our
> wounds constraining—
> and so its life with praise is shining,
> rousing and reviving all.[5]

A Revolving Circle of Glory

Shared glory and mutual glorification is a key feature of the Trinity. Christian life—and prayer—means to be drawn into the life (and prayer) of the Trinity: "one degree of glory to another."

The relationships, the rhythms, in the life of the Trinity mark out a path of glory. The Spirit belongs to that "revolving circle of glory moving from like to like" between the Father, the Spirit, and the Son. And the Spirit provides the entrance into this circle of glory. Human beings lack the full capacity to glorify God. "Of ourselves," Basil writes, "we are not capable of giving glory, but in the Spirit we have the aptitude." That's because the Spirit lives in the rich and perfect communion of the Father and the Son, and "only the Spirit can adequately glorify the Lord." Basil uses an analogy: when objects are placed near something brilliant and glorious, they themselves begin to take on something of that glory; so it is that the "glory of the Spirit is changed into [the believer's] glory, not stingily, or dimly, but with abundance."[6]

Gregory of Nyssa saw the glory of God working at three levels: among the three members of the Trinity; between the Trinity and human beings; and among human beings themselves in the community of faith. The experience of divine glory creates a deep and inner unity—perfectly within the Trinity and partially with those who are drawn into that circle of glory by the Spirit. Christians "repeat [the circle] in prayer, glorifying the Son by means of the Spirit, and the Father by means of the Son."[7]

Similarly, Basil appropriates the rich biblical imagery used in the praise of God: beauty, light, joy, grandeur, splendor, radiance, and dance. Though the divine glory defies language, such images open the doorway into praise of God.

We seek to behold "the beauty of the Lord" and to reflect this beauty back before the ugliness and brokenness of our world. This beauty—centered in the beauty of Christ—becomes visible as Christ is formed in the community of God's people through the work of the Spirit. Scripture talks about reflecting God's glory. Father, Spirit, and Son, sharing perfect love and holiness, form a "revolving circle of glory." Through the Spirit we are invited into—drawn into—that experience of glory. Through the Spirit we can move from one degree of glory to another, reflecting the glory, the beauty, of the Lord.

Thomas Smail writes, "In the Son the glory of the Father becomes incarnate among us, in the Spirit that same glory becomes experiential within us."[8] The Spirit's work is to create glory within us, and to glorify us together with Christ—that is, to transform us so that we become glorious. "If you are insulted because of the name of Christ, you are blessed, for the Spirit of glory and of God rests upon you" (1 Pet. 4:14). 1 Peter 4:13 speaks of a coming time when the full glory of the ascended Christ will be revealed to believers. In the meantime, in the midst of reproaches for the name of Christ, the same Spirit who rested on the Messiah and who reveals his glory will rest continuously on them.

This glorification of believers has begun. Through the Spirit we are already being changed from one degree of glory to another as we gaze on the face of the Lord (2 Cor. 3:17–18). The completion of this glorification awaits the Spirit's ministry in the resurrection. Paul attributes Christ's resurrection to the Spirit, though in a somewhat nuanced way (Rom. 1:4; Rom. 8:11; cf. 1 Tim. 3:16). Paul says that Christ was raised from the dead by the "*glory* of the Father" (Rom. 6:4), which may well be an allusion to the work of the Spirit. Christ's resurrection into a body of glory forms the prototype of the resurrection body of all believers. In the resurrection body, the power or energies of the Spirit are fully released.

In the present, the Spirit rests on and dwells in believers, and they are energized and empowered in the midst of their weakness (2 Cor. 12:9–10; 13:4; Phil. 4:13). The frailty of the flesh and the life/energy of the Spirit coalesce. The Spirit's transforming life is experienced in and through a still disordered creation, a creation subject to "frustration" and "groaning." But even now the Spirit is creating glory within us, and with the "redemption of our bodies" (Rom. 8:23), the Spirit's work will enable full participation in the "freedom and glory of the children of God" (8:21). Creation itself will be freed from its bondage to decay and share fully in the glorious liberty of God's children (8:21).[9]

In the Spirit, the glorification of believers has begun.

The *Abba* Experience

Near the heart of the Christian life is the *Abba* experience, a new intimacy with God made possible by the death of Jesus and the witness of the Spirit.

We have become children of God, adopted into the family of God, heirs of God and co-heirs with Christ. The metaphor of adoption pictures Jesus' death as bringing people into God's family. The Greek term for adoption means "to be in the Son's place."[10] Christians are God's adopted sons and daughters, a surprising and rich metaphor pointing both to family membership and a new legal status. It appears in five New Testament passages (Rom. 8:15; 8:23; 9:14; Gal. 4:4–5; Eph. 1:5–7). One of these passages explicitly relates adoption to Christ's death: "in love he predestined us for adoption to sonship through Jesus Christ. . . . In him we have redemption through his blood, the forgiveness of sins in accordance with the riches of God's grace" (Eph. 1:5–7).

Two other of these passages speak of God as *Abba*, emphasizing the depth and intimacy of relationship that Christ's death makes possible. When we cry, *Abba*! Father! it is the Spirit himself bearing witness with our Spirit that we are children of God (Rom. 8:15–16); and "God sent the Spirit of his Son into our hearts, the Spirit who calls out, '*Abba*, Father'" (Gal. 4:6). In both texts, the Spirit's crying *Abba* is the clear sign for Christians that they are sons and daughters of God and fellow heirs with Christ (Rom. 8:17–18; Gal. 4:7).

This Aramaic word was likely retained by the earliest Christians because it was characteristic of the prayer of Jesus. They were confident of sharing sonship with him because they shared the *Abba* prayer with him. *Abba* was likely Jesus' characteristic way of praying. It was a term of family intimacy, an intimacy that Jesus' experienced in deep ways with his Father.[11] "*Abba*, Father," he said, "everything is possible for you. Take this cup from me. Yet not what I will, but what you will" (Mark 14:36). This intimacy is seen in other statements: "No one knows who the Son is except the Father, and no one knows who the Father is except the Son and those to whom the Son chooses to reveal him" (Lk. 10:22).

Paul uses the adoption metaphor in a strong Trinitarian pattern. He writes to the Galatians: "God sent his Son . . . that we might receive the full rights [adoption] of sons. Because you are sons, God sent the Spirit of his Son into our hearts, the Spirit who calls out, '*Abba*, Father'" (Gal. 4:4–6). Here the same movement that is attributed to the Son (Gal. 4:4) is also attributed to the Spirit: God sent his Son and God sent the Spirit of his Son. God, the Son, and the Spirit are all involved in the determination to bring about the sonship of the Galatians. Because the Spirit joins in the Son's cry of "*Abba*, Father!," the Galatians also participate in that cry. "The Spirit is the corroborating evidence of their sonship, their adoptive relationship with the Father through the Son." Adoption is an act of the Trinity: "the Father adopts strangers by uniting them to Christ by the Spirit through faith."[12]

It's an astounding Christian truth—that when we become followers of Jesus we become daughters and sons of the Father, right alongside Jesus the beloved Son. He was a Son by birthright; we by adoption into the family. He was God's heir; we become co-heirs.

For many of us—at least many that I know, including myself—the experienced reality of this truth comes hard and slow. Harsh or distant fathers have set up in their sons and daughters a deep sense of disapproval and an almost unquenchable hunger for affirmation and approval. This was the overriding quest of Henri Nouwen that he chronicled in many popular books. A pivotal text for Nouwen was the descent of the Spirit upon Jesus at the Jordan River, with the Father's words, "You are my Beloved!" "Everything that Jesus said or did came forth from that most intimate spiritual communion." And we too "are invited to that same communion that Jesus lived, that we are the beloved sons and daughters of God just as he is the Beloved Son, that we are sent into the world to proclaim the belovedness of all people as he was." But this identity as the beloved easily slips away from us, so life in Christ requires "a constant claiming of our true identity." "The question is not 'How am I to love God?' but 'How am I to let myself be loved by God?'" "Dear friend," he wrote to a skeptic, "being the Beloved is the origin and the fulfillment of the life of the Spirit." Over and over, Nouwen's basic message was the same: "You are God's Beloved!"[13]

Popular author Brennan Manning, like Nouwen, tells of his long journey to receive the Father's love. "For eighteen years," he wrote, "I proclaimed the good news of God's passionate, unconditional love—utterly convinced in my head but not feeling it in my heart." During a season of spiritual collapse and desolation, he began walking with a counselor and spiritual guide. Then, on the tenth day of a mostly solitary retreat deep in the mountains of Colorado, he experienced a breakthrough. Through a flood of tears, he said, "in the distance I heard music and dancing . . . Jesus removed the shroud of perfectionist thinking, and now forgiven and free, I ran home. . . . Gripped in the depths of my soul, tears streaming down my checks, I internalized and finally felt all the words I had written and spoken about stubborn, relentless Love. . . . I leaped from simply being the teacher of God's love to becoming Abba's delight." Since that experience, Manning's constant charge became, "Today on Planet Earth, you may experience the wonder and beauty of yourself as Abba's child and temple of the Holy Spirit through Jesus Christ our Lord."[14]

The Spirit of God enables our spirits to soar as we come to experience God as the one whom Jesus called *Abba*.

Refreshment for Mission

In his public ministry, Jesus exhibits the ebb and flow of solitude and public ministry, of prayer and proclamation. He goes into the towns, among the crowds, then back to the mountain or the garden to pray. He teaches, heals, and eats with all kinds of people, and then goes away with his disciples for a while. Or early in the morning while it's still dark, he goes to pray. It's a steady movement from solitude and stillness to action and ministry.

And so it is with us. "As a healthy organism breathes in and breathes out," Scott Sundquist writes, "so the church goes out in mission and returns to receive needed oxygen in community worship."[15] In and out—inward in drawing close to God in worship, outward in serving as agents of *shalom* in a disordered world. Mission and worship, mission and life in the Spirit are deeply intertwined.

Peace and Joy in the Holy Spirit

Joy and peace flow out of the growing and deepening experience of God's glory and the life-reorienting experience of God as *Abba*.

Joy and peace are fruit of the Spirit (Gal. 5). "The kingdom of God is not a matter of eating and drinking, but of righteousness, peace and joy in the Holy Spirit" (Rom. 14:17). "May the God of hope fill you with all joy and peace as you trust in him, so that you may overflow in hope by the power of the Holy Spirit" (Rom. 15:13). In the midst of severe suffering, the Thessalonians experienced "the joy given by the Holy Spirit" (1 Thess. 1:6). And Peter, writing to beleaguered exiles, said, "you believe in him and are filled with an inexpressible and glorious joy" (1 Pet. 1:8)

"Christ has come to bring joy," Miroslav Volf said, "not only by turning darkness into light, conquering powers of evil, and establishing the reign of justice. He has also come to bring joy by turning water into wine, by overcoming what we lack, and helping sustain and enhance the goods we already enjoy."[16]

In the Spirit on the Lord's Day

As we saw in the previous chapter, the worshipping assembly is a uniquely intense place of the Spirit's empowering presence. There the Spirit enables us to enter more deeply into "union" with Christ, into the very life of God, the Trinity. Paul cited scripture [Isaiah 64] that speaks of things beyond our seeing, things beyond our hearing, things beyond our imagining, all prepared by God for those who love him. He clearly believed that what Isaiah envisioned had become reality in the messianic gift of the Spirit (1 Cor. 2:9, 10). There was a deep, unspeakable relation here. We can call it a kind of ecstatic intimacy with God, a being caught up out of ourselves.

When the people of God are "in the Spirit" on the Lord's Day, they are caught up into the heavenly sanctuary. We draw near, not to Mount Sinai (Exod. 19–24) but to Mount Zion, "the heavenly Jerusalem, . . . to thousands upon thousands of angels in joyful assembly, to the church of the firstborn . . . to God the judge of all, . . . and to Jesus" (Heb. 12:22–24). In worship we join the end-time assembly—we "see" and experience God's future; we join the end-time celebration of saints from every tribe, language, and nation; and we are refreshed and strengthened to live in the dawning of this future. This is part of the glorification that God intends, participating in that "circle of glory" opened up to us through the Spirit.

The same Spirit who draws us into the "glory" of God's own life also draws us into fellowship with our sisters and brothers in Christ. We experience the "fellowship of the Holy Spirit." This fellowship means "participation *in* nearness to God *with* others in whom the same Spirit works."[17] This is the normal work of the Spirit. It is how we get refreshed and filled with "all joy and peace in believing."

Surveying the vast spectrum of churches and movements that make up global Pentecostalism, James McClendon sought its broader meaning and message. "The highly visible ecstasy-and-fellowship of Pentecostals," he suggested, "is the Spirit's fresh signal that ecstasy and fellowship are the distinguishing marks of the Spirit of God." What all Christians can learn is that "the reality of present enjoyment in the Christian life, of Spirit-given full salvation now (albeit only a rich foretaste of eternal salvation) is fully claimed and rightly shared by all who bow the knee to Jesus Christ as Lord."[18]

When we assemble in the Spirit on the Lord's Day, we enter the temple of God's presence. Through the Spirit we experience that presence. There we can stand on tiptoe, as it were, to see more of God's future, the new creation coming. There we partake of resurrection life. "When the Spirit of the resurrection is experienced," Moltmann declares, "a person breathes freely again, and gets up out of the defeats and anxieties of his or her life. People lift up their heads, possessed by the indescribable joy that we find in the Easter hymns."[19]

Living in the rhythm of worship and witness, of gathering and sending, we find strength and refreshment to live our lives on mission.

NOTES

[1] John R. Levison, *Filled with the Spirit* (Grand Rapids: Eerdmans, 2009), 88.

[2] Levison, *Filled with the Spirit*, 253–66.

[3] Levison, *Filled with the Spirit*, 263.

[4] Jürgen Moltmann, *The Spirit of Life* (Minneapolis: Fortress, 1992), 274, 275, 276, 278.

[5] Hildegard of Bingen (d. 1136), "Spiritus Sanctus Vivificans," trans. Nathaniel M. Campbell, International Society of Hildegard von Bingen Studies (website), accessed February 3, 2018, http://www.hildegard-society.org/2014/11/spiritus-sanctus-vivificans-antiphon.html.

[6] Basil, *On the Holy Spirit*, 26.63; 27.68; 21.52.

[7] Gregory of Nyssa, *Against the Macedonians* 22, cited by Kilian McDonnell, *The Other Hand of God: The Holy Spirit as the Universal Touch and Goal* (Collegeville, MN: Liturgical Press, 2003), 25, 26.

[8] Thomas Smail, *Reflected Glory: The Spirit in Christ and in Christians* (London, UK: Hodder, 1975), 46.

[9] Paul's vision of the future in Romans envisions not the destruction and recreation of the cosmos, but its liberation and renewal. And Peter speaks of the emergence of "a new heaven and a new earth" (2 Pet. 3:10–13). Heaven and earth, it appears, will form one realm of righteousness where the Spirit of God will pervade the atmosphere. God will be "all in all" (1 Cor. 15:28).

[10] See Trevor J. Burke, *Adopted into God's Family: Exploring a Pauline Metaphor* (Downers Grove, IL: InterVarsity, 2007).

[11] When Jeremias called the use of *Abba* Jesus' most important linguistic innovation, he was overstating his case, though we can still say that the word was characteristic of Jesus' prayer life and that it conveyed a sense of intimacy with God that was distinctive among his contemporaries. Joachim Jeremias, *The Prayers of Jesus* (Naperville, IL: Allenson, 1967), 58–63; James D. G. Dunn, *Jesus and the Spirit: A Study of the Religious and Charismatic Experience of Jesus and the First Christians as Reflected in the New Testament* (Grand Rapids: Eerdmans, 1997), 20–40.

[12] Wesley Hill, *Paul and the Trinity: Persons, Relations, and the Pauline Letters* (Grand Rapids: Eerdmans, 2015), 143; Kevin Vanhoozer, *Jesus, Paul, and the People of God* (Downers Grove, IL: InterVarsity, 2011), 256.

[13] Henri Nouwen, *Here and Now: Living in the Spirit* (New York: Crossroad, 1994), 135–36; *Return of the Prodigal: A Story of Homecoming* (New York: Doubleday, 1992), 100; *Life of the Beloved: Spiritual Living in a Secular World* (New York: Crossroad, 1992), 37.

[14] Brennan Manning, *Abba's Child: The Cry of the Heart for Intimate Belonging* (1994; Colorado Springs: NavPress, 2015), 10, xvii.

[15] Scott Sundquist, *Understanding Christian Mission: Participation in Suffering and Glory* (Grand Rapids: Baker Academic, 2013), 281.

[16] Miroslav Volf, "Joy Is for Epiphany, Too," *Christian Century*, December 27, 2017, https://www.christiancentury.org/article/critical-essay/joy-epiphany-too.

[17] James McClendon, *Systematic Theology, Volume 2: Doctrine* (Nashville: Abingdon, 1994), 443.

[18] McClendon, *Systematic Theology, Volume 2*, 437–38.

[19] Jürgen Moltmann, *The Source of Life: The Holy Spirit and the Theology of Life* (Minneapolis: Fortress, 1997), 31.

8

GROANING

> In the midst of a groaning creation and our own groaning, the Spirit intercedes on our behalf with wordless groaning.

We ourselves, who have the firstfruits of the Spirit, groan inwardly as we wait eagerly for . . . the redemption of our bodies. . . . the Spirit himself intercedes for us through wordless groans.
—Romans 8:23, 26b

Cruciformity is Paul's all-encompassing spirituality. It is the modus operandi *of life in Christ.*
—Michael Gorman

How does life in the Spirit relate to pain and failure, dereliction and desolation, testing and trial? What about the times when, according to Paul, we "groan and are burdened"—and our groans join with those of the creation itself? And what about Paul's disconcerting invitation to let the Spirit draw us into sharing the passion, the sufferings, of Christ?

Is this part of life in the Spirit? Or is the Spirit mostly about joy, fullness, exuberance, and "soaring"? Is the Spirit only "a 'triumphalist' Spirit, bearer of joy and positive 'feeling'?" Or must one "not allow as much for the fire of purgation as for the refreshment of the comforting dove?"[1] Such questions are the focus of this chapter.

Groaning between the Times

The apostle Paul wrote: "we ourselves, who have the firstfruits of the Spirit, groan inwardly as we wait eagerly for . . . the redemption of our bodies. . . . the Spirit himself intercedes for us with groans that words cannot express" (Rom. 8:23, 26b). Paul begins this section by contrasting "our present sufferings" with "the glory that will be revealed in us" (8:18); "we boast in the hope of the glory of God," and "we also glory in our sufferings" (5:2–3).

Central here is Paul's overarching eschatological framework—the bold "already" and the steady awareness of the "not yet"—in which the Spirit plays the central role (as we saw in Chapter Four). The Christian lives "between the times," and part of this life between the times, is groaning. We have already received adoption into God's family, as the Spirit enables us to cry, "*Abba*, Father," yet we groan in waiting for that adoption (Rom. 8:15, 23). We possess the Spirit as the first fruits of the coming harvest, yet at the same time, we groan, and the Spirit intercedes, as we wait for that final harvest (8:23). Paul makes a similar point in 2 Corinthians: "we groan and are burdened," eager for the resurrection body so that "what is mortal may be swallowed up by life" (2 Cor. 5:4). In the midst of this groaning, we claim "the Spirit as a deposit, guaranteeing what is to come" (2 Cor. 5:5).

This groaning has a cosmic dimension. Our groanings are in solidarity with the groanings of the created order, which has been "subjected to frustration" and waits with "eager longing" (Rom. 8:19). And so "the whole creation has been groaning as in the pains of childbirth," longing to be freed from its "bondage to decay" (8:21–22). Its redemption is related to that of God's sons and daughters; it longs to share in the same freedom and glory of those who live the life of the Spirit. So Paul can include the nonhuman world; there will be cosmic redemption along with human redemption. He does not consider the body separate from the rest of creation. Like the redeemed body, creation itself will be transformed and in its own way glorified, not cast aside as unnecessary scaffolding.

After describing the groaning and eager longing of creation and how we join in that groaning, Paul makes a surprising turn to the role of the Spirit in this groaning. "The Spirit helps us in our weakness. We do not

know what we ought to pray for, but the Spirit himself intercedes for us"
(Rom. 8:26). The Spirit assists us in our weakness by praying to the Father
on our behalf with "wordless groans." It's a difficult phrase to get a handle
on. It is sometimes rendered "inexpressible," "inarticulate," or "too deep
for words." Is the Spirit praying through us while we pray, or does the
Spirit pray while we keep silent? Does "wordless" or "inarticulate" indicate
silence, or does it indicate sounds that are not recognizable or understood
by the mind?

Some interpret what is going on here as private silent prayer in which
the Spirit is simply assisting our own praying—because we "do not know
what to pray for"—and that it is not really groaning at all. Others point to
this as one form of "praying in the Spirit," reflecting Paul's exhortation to
"pray in the Spirit on all occasions with all kinds of prayers" (Eph. 6:18; cf.
1 Cor. 14:15, where he contrasts two ways of praying—with the mind and
with the S/spirit). In this reading, Paul could well have in mind a kind of
private praying in tongues that requires no public interpretation. In this
view, "wordless groaning" would not mean "silent" or "inexpressible" but
closer to "inarticulate"—where the Spirit joins us in our groaning to make
his appeal on our behalf.[2] In either case, because God knows the mind of
the Spirit—they share a life of perfect love and oneness—we can be assured
that this prayer is "in accordance with the will of God" and "for God's
people" (Rom. 8:27).

Another way to approach Romans 8 and the Spirit's groaning with and
for us is to see prayer as entering into the life of the Trinity. In this view,
Romans 8 gives us a glimpse of the prayer going on within the life of God.
An intimate conversation goes on everlastingly as part of the self-giving
love and deep mutuality in the Trinity. The Spirit invites and enables us
to join in. We could say that prayer is being drawn into the communion
already going on among the Father, Son, and Spirit. So Paul is describing
deep prayer in the Spirit ("sighs too deep for words"). With this Trinitarian
communion in view, Sarah Coakley says, commenting on Romans 8:26, "it
is not I who autonomously prays, but God (the Holy Spirit) who prays in
me, and so answers the eternal call of the 'Father,' drawing me by various
painful degrees into the newly expanded life of 'Sonship.'"[3]

Paul lived, like us, between suffering and glory. He experienced real hardship and suffering, and times when he almost despaired of life itself (2 Cor. 1:8–9, 11). But he could say that "our present sufferings are not worth comparing with the glory that will be revealed in us" (Rom. 8:18). Between the suffering and the glory—that's where the groaning comes from. In that location, it has three dimensions:

1. A cry of pain, sorrow, and disappointment at the way things are;
2. A groan of eager longing for God's new creation; and
3. An act of intercession for the coming of that future.[4]

The groaning is at the same time a cry of grief over the present conditions and a prayer for new creation. In this groaning with and for us, the Spirit is "praying creation into glory," and melding our groaning with the Spirit's groaning as a means of prayer to the Father. The groaning and the glory belong together. Just ten verses later, Paul can declare triumphantly that "we are more than conquerors through him who loved us" and that nothing in all creation can separate us from the love of God in Christ (Rom. 8:37, 39).

The Spirit is not simply "personal" but more than personal—"supra-personal" as we saw in Chapter Three. So the Spirit has a depth of personal range; we might say that the Spirit searches and knows us in ways more profound than we know ourselves—one who knows the "secrets of human beings" (Rom. 2:16), "searches all things" (1 Cor. 2:10), and probes our weakness with empathetic groans or sighs too deep for words (Rom. 8:26).

The Spirit of God suffers with the suffering, and draws near to the powerless and inarticulate. As Moltmann notes, "Even if people can do no more than sigh for redemption, and then fall dumb even as they sigh, God's Spirit already sighs within them and intercedes for them." When the Spirit comes to indwell "wandering and suffering created beings, the Spirit thrusts forward with intense longing for union with God, and sighs to be at rest in the new, perfected creation."[5]

A stanza from an ancient hymn by Bianco da Siena (d. fifteenth century) captures something of this depth and mystery:

And so the yearning strong, with which the soul will long,
Shall far outpass the power of human telling;
For none can guess its grace, till he become the place
Wherein the Holy Spirit makes His dwelling.[6]

The Spirit and Cruciformity

The shape of the Christian life, for Paul, is cruciform or cross-shaped: "The life I now live in the body, I live by faith in the Son of God, who loved me and gave himself for me" (Gal. 2:20b). Michael Gorman argues that "cruciformity is Paul's all-encompassing spirituality. It is the *modus operandi* of life in Christ."[7] It means self-giving, power in weakness, suffering, even a kind of co-crucifixion with Christ (Gal. 2:20a). Christian life is shaped by the character and example of Jesus. It is the work of the Spirit to incorporate us—to train us—into that life.

The cross of Jesus is the ultimate demonstration of God's power and wisdom, though in the eyes of the world's wisdom it is madness and folly (1 Cor. 1:18–25). The people of this present age who are pursuing wisdom and who consider the cross to be folly cannot understand true wisdom because they do not possess the Spirit of God.

In Christ's crucifixion, God demonstrated the divine power (1 Cor. 1:22–24), and through the Spirit, who is the Spirit of the crucified Messiah, continues to demonstrate that power in and through the community of Christ.

But the Spirit's power is not what we may think or gladly seek. Yes, the Spirit brings us into union with Christ and intimacy with the Father (*Abba*), and strengthens us in our weakness. Yet there are two hard realities.

First, through the body of Christ, the Spirit has an "active killing function." Through the Spirit something is put to death. Paul says, "if by the Spirit you put to death the misdeeds of the body, you will live" (Rom. 8:13). "Through the Spirit what took place decisively in the death of Christ continually takes place: the believer dies to the old life 'according to the flesh.'" This is because the "believer is still part of an untransformed world and through the body is subject to the attack of the old powers. In the face of such attacks, the believer's past death with Christ [in baptism] must be maintained and affirmed in the present."[8] The Spirit-filled believer is not a passive bystander in this process; rather, the Spirit enables the dying process if and as we open ourselves to it and actively participate in the process.

Second, the Spirit enables believers to suffer with Christ. "Now if we are [God's] children, then we are heirs—heirs of God and co-heirs with Christ, if indeed, we share in his sufferings in order that we may also share in his glory" (Rom. 8:17). The Spirit connects believers to the cross, where they become marked by conformity to Christ's death. They become people of self-giving, self-sacrificing love. So, as Gorman argues, the *"criterion of the Spirit's activity is cruciformity, understood as Christ-like love in the edification of others rather than oneself"* (italics original).[9]

Paul does not see a basic contradiction between a dynamic life in the Spirit and the experience of suffering and weakness (see 2 Cor. 11–13; Rom. 8:26; 1 Cor. 2:3, 15:43). He can "delight in weaknesses, in insults, in hardships, in persecutions, in difficulties" (2 Cor. 12:10). He can do this because such experiences point to Christ who was "crucified in weakness, yet he lives by God's power" (2 Cor. 13:4). Suffering is interpreted eschatologically—it produces perseverance, well-formed character, and hope, all because the Spirit has poured God's love into our hearts (Rom. 5:2–5). And Paul can even describe the suffering as "light and momentary troubles" (2 Cor. 4:17).

For Paul and the New Testament, the life in Christ—which is always a life on mission in the Spirit-filled community—inescapably involves suffering, an identification with Christ in his death. The suffering in mind here is not primarily the ills and vicissitudes of life but rather missional suffering—pressure, opposition, and persecution. Public witness to Christ and to God's new and inbreaking kingdom usually generates distaste, harassment, scorn, opposition, or worse.

The other New Testament writings set forth a similar perspective. In Acts, much hardship and suffering comes as the gospel challenges, by word and by deed, the ruling powers of the day. Persecution quickly breaks out in Jerusalem (Acts 3–4; 8:1). Stephen was a witness led by the Spirit (6:5, 10; 7:55), but it resulted in his martyrdom; through the Spirit he sees heaven opened and the Son of Man standing at the right hand of God as if to welcome him. The Spirit who enabled him to witness and to see into heaven also enabled him to face death. After the conversion of Saul, the Lord (through Ananias) says, "I will show him how much he must suffer for my name" (9:16). Later, after being stoned in Lystra, Paul (with Barnabas) admonished the disciples of the region: "We must go through many hardships to enter the kingdom of God" (14:22). These hardships become regular occurrences throughout the rest of Paul's story (13:50; 14:4–6, 19; 16:19–24; 17:5, 32; 18:6; 19:23–40; 21:30–36; 23:12–15; 27:14–28:5).

In short, in the story told in Acts, "to be led by the Spirit assumes the possibility, indeed the probability, of suffering." In Acts, the mission of God and suffering are closely connected. "Clearly suffering is a major force in the gospel's expansion. It is a rare thing for the Way to spread without it. . . . Certainly the gospel moves, but never without pain."[10]

For the strangers and exiles addressed by Peter, the charge is similar: "To this you were called, because Christ suffered for you, leaving you an example, that you should follow in his steps" (1 Pet. 2:21). "Therefore since Christ suffered in his body, arm yourselves also with the same attitude, because whoever suffers in the body is done with sin. As a result, they do not live the rest of their earthly lives for evil human desires but rather for the will of God" (1 Pet. 4:1–2).

Praise and Lament in the Spirit

The eschatological framework of the New Testament, which we have touched on repeatedly throughout this book, frames both our joy in the Spirit and our groaning in the Spirit. The bold "already" alongside the ever-present "not yet" gives Christians an "odd capacity for simultaneous joy amidst suffering and impatience with things as they are."[11]

If our praise to God is Spirit empowered, what about our groaning or lament? Why is lament seldom a feature of worship in many churches? "Modern evangelical worship," Robin Parry observed, "is uncompromisingly happy and those present engage weekly in declaring how thankful and joyful they feel about God."[12] Can joy and exuberant praise be joined in the rhythms of worship with lament—the cry for the fulfillment of new creation?

Far from an act of weak faith or lack of faith, lament in Scripture is an act of bold faith. The very struggles, grief, and suffering that would seem to drive believers away from God are the very things that are brought before God. Lament gives voice to grief, forsakenness, and anger. But it is more than that. It is also a prayer—a cry—for God to act, to deliver, to intervene. It is a kind of intercessory prayer, aided by the Spirit.

Jesus provides an example for us. Shortly before he died, he cried out with a loud voice, "My God, my God, why have you forsaken me?" It was a quotation from Psalm 22—a lament psalm, which Jesus undoubtedly knew well. He likely intended those words to point to the message of the whole psalm. The psalmist proceeds to detail the mockery and misery of his plight (Ps. 22:6–18), and then asks the Lord to deliver him from "the mouth of lions" (22:21). Then he concludes: "For the Lord has not despised or scorned the sufferings of his afflicted one; he has not hidden his face from him but has listened to his cry for help" (22:24).

What was the Spirit doing on the Friday when Jesus uttered this cry of lament? I submit that the Spirit was doing what the Spirit had been doing since coming to rest on Jesus at the Jordan—empowering him to carry out the messianic mission, enabling him to face temptation, sustaining him in his ordeal. With Jesus on the cross, the Spirit was sharing in his suffering, groaning with him in his agony and his lament, lifting up this groaning as prayer in the unbroken fellowship of the Trinity.

In a similar way, our prayers—including our cries of lament—are offered to the Father, through Jesus the Son, in the power of the Holy Spirit. We are to pray in the Spirit, says Paul, with all kinds of prayers. The prayer of lament is one of them.

"Blessed are those who mourn," Jesus said, "for they will be comforted" (Matt. 5:4). We ask: Who are the mourners? "The Mourners are those who have caught a glimpse of God's new day, who ache with all their being for that day's coming, and who break out into tears when confronted by its absence." "The mourners are aching visionaries."[13] The mourners are all of us who follow Jesus in the power of the Spirit.

The Realities of Mission

As we have seen, the fledgling church in the New Testament faced pressure and danger at every turn as the Holy Spirit prompted and guided them on Jesus' mission. This was the reality of the mission of Christ. Paul knew that reality better than anyone, which is why he could write this astounding litany describing his ministry:

> We recommend ourselves as God's servants: with much patience, with suffering, difficulties, hardships, beatings, imprisonments, riots, hard work, sleepless nights, going without food, with purity, knowledge, great-heartedness, kindness, the Holy Spirit, genuine love, by speaking the truth, by God's power, with weapons for God's faithful work in left and right hand alike, through glory and shame, through slander and praise; as deceivers, and yet true; as unknown, yet very well known; as dying, and look—we are alive; as punished, yet not killed; as sad, yet always celebrating; as poor, yet bringing riches to many; as having nothing, yet possessing everything. (2 Cor. 6:4–10 KNT)

Paul had experienced "soaring," in the Spirit, by God's power, with love and joy and glory; and he had experienced manifold "groaning," in hardships, prison, sleeplessness, hunger, slander, sadness, and poverty. All of it was part of life in the Spirit on his mission to the Gentiles.

Though Jesus through his death and resurrection has already won the decisive victory over the powers that bully, oppress, and enslave people, those powers seek to keep this world in their own grip. They fight back when their hold on things is challenged. So it should be expected that disciples on mission encounter opposition. The working out of Jesus' victory involves disciples who are identified with Jesus in his suffering. That's what our baptism means—we died with Jesus, and through the Spirit's "active killing function" continue to put to death the old person and put on the new person in Christ. So "following Jesus will mean disappointment, failure, frustration, muddle, misunderstanding, pain, and sorrow—and those are just the 'first-world problems.'"[14] The "two-thirds world" challenges may run harder. All of these things come, in various ways and times, on the path of discipleship and mission because this is how the kingdom of God comes. Not by the way of might and control but by the very way of Jesus—sacrificial, covenant love.

In this way, the "sufferings of Jesus's followers—of the whole Body of Christ, now in one member, now in another—brings the victory of the cross into fresh reality, so that fresh outpourings of that victory may emerge."[15] The *victory* of the cross gets worked out through the *way* of the cross. The mission of Christ, in the power of the Spirit, involves the way of sacrificial love. That is the way God's kingdom comes. That is why the Spirit pours God's love into our hearts.

Lesslie Newbigin, a foremost missional theologian in the twentieth century, observed that "During the long centuries of the 'Constantinian era' of church history, when Christians have normally had the authority of the state behind them, it has been regarded as abnormal that Christians should suffer for their faith." Many Christians have thereby taken it for granted that one should be able to go anywhere and preach Christ and be protected by the law. But "neither Scripture nor common sense provides any foundation" for this assumption. He adds that the "New Testament makes it plain that Christ's followers must expect suffering as the normal badge of their discipleship, and also as one of the characteristic forms of their witness."[16]

Jürgen Moltman, speaking of the "apostolic" mark of the church (one of the four Nicene marks), said, "Participation in the apostolic mission of Christ therefore leads inescapably into tribulation, contradiction and suffering. The apostolate is carried out in the weakness and poverty of Christ, not through force or the strategies of force."[17]

This biblical truth is very difficult for comfortable Western Christians to really fathom. No doubt it was also difficult for the earliest Christians to fathom at first. But "tribulation, contradiction, and suffering" became a steady reality as the faith slowly spread across the Roman world—from social scorn to legal pressures to physical suffering and death. Even so, the church's greatest growth came in the latter part of the third century, a time when social pressures and threat of persecution were high.

Still, the challenges and perils of Christ's mission are apparent all around us. In 1998, ten twentieth-century Christian martyrs were commemorated with statues in Westminster Abbey. These ten were chosen as representatives of the persecution and oppression of Christians from every continent. They all died for their Christian beliefs, victims of Nazism, racism, Communism, and religious persecution of various sorts. They are Maximilian Kolbe (Poland), Manche Masemola (South Africa), Janani Luwum (Uganda), Grand Duchess Elizabeth (Russia), Martin Luther King Jr. (United States), Óscar Romero (El Salvador), Dietrich Bonhoeffer (Germany), Esther John (Pakistan), Lucian Tapiedi (New Guinea), and Wang Zhiming (China). They represent a huge host of Christian believers martyred for the faith in different parts of the world in the twentieth century.[18]

More recently (2017), we've heard about the twenty-one Coptic Christians publicly beheaded on a beach in North Africa, some of whom shouted "Jesus!" as they died. Many others were raped, tortured, and shot. They are all martyrs and witnesses. And for every story in the headlines, there are hundreds of other stories.

In this disorienting time between the times, we sigh and groan for the redemption of our bodies and for the completion of God's new creation—a groaning, we might say, heightened by the very foretaste and assurance of God's coming reign that the Spirit provides us.

We believe that God, through the Spirit, is in charge of the events of human history and that in Christ all things will be summed up—for the Spirit is the "guarantee of our inheritance until we acquire possession of it" (Eph. 1:14). In the Spirit we share in the groaning and travail of creation, but this groaning is filled with hope because the Spirit assures us that we are adopted children of God and heirs with Christ (Rom. 8:14–25).

The church, as it engages in the mission of God, is not promised success; but "it is promised the peace of Christ in the midst of tribulation, and the witness of the Spirit given out of the church's weakness and ignorance."[19]

NOTES

[1] Sarah Coakley, *God, Sexuality, and the Self: An Essay "On the Trinity"* (Cambridge, UK: Cambridge University, 2013), 180, 181.

[2] For this second view, see Gordon Fee, *God's Empowering Presence* (Peabody, MA: Hendrickson, 1994), 575–86; Krister Stendahl, *Paul among Jews and Gentiles* (London: SCM, 1977), 109–24; and Gerd Theissen, *Psychological Aspects of Pauline Theology* (1987; reprint edition, Minneapolis: Fortress, 1999).

[3] Coakley, *God, Sexuality, and the Self*, 55-56.

[4] Robin Parry, *Worshipping Trinity: Coming Back to the Heart of Worship*, 2nd edition (Eugene, OR: Cascade, 2012), 140.

[5] Jürgen Moltmann, *The Spirit of Life: A Universal Affirmation* (Minneapolis: Fortress, 1992), 51.

[6] Bianco da Siena, "Come Down, O Love Divine," translated by Richard Littledale; *United Methodist Hymnal* (Nashville: Abingdon, 1989).

[7] Michael Gorman, *Reading Paul* (Eugene, OR: Cascade, 2008), 147. See also his major work, *Cruciformity: Paul's Narrative Spirituality of the Cross* (Grand Rapids: Eerdmans, 2001).

[8] Robert C. Tannehill, *Dying and Rising with Christ: A Study in Pauline Theology* (Berlin: Topelmann, 1966), 80.

[9] Gorman, *Cruciformity*, 57–62, 60. See also Charles H. Cosgrove, *The Cross and the Spirit: A Study in the Argument and Theology of Galatians* (Macon, GA: Mercer University, 1988), 169–94.

[10] Keith Warrington, "Suffering and the Spirit in Luke-Acts," *Journal of Biblical and Pneumatological Research* 1 (2009): 29; Paul House, "Suffering and the Purpose of Acts," *Journal of the Evangelical Theological Society* 33, no. 3 (September 1990): 326.

[11] Richard Hays, *The Moral Vision of the New Testament: A Contemporary Introduction to New Testament Ethics* (New York: HarperCollins, 1996),198.

[12] Parry, *Worshipping Trinity*, 142.

[13] Nicholas Wolterstorff, *Lament for a Son* (Grand Rapids: Eerdmans, 1987), 85–86.

[14] N. T. Wright, *The Day the Revolution Began* (New York: HarperCollins, 2016), 410.

[15] Wright, *The Day the Revolution Began*, 369.

[16] Lesslie Newbigin, *Trinitarian Doctrine for Today's Mission* (1988; Wipf & Stock, 2006), 46.

[17] Jürgen Moltmann, *The Church in the Power of the Spirit* (Minneapolis: Fortress, 1993), 361.

[18] The Pew Research Center prepares an annual update on "Latest Trends in Religious Restrictions and Hostilities," which ranks 198 countries and territories by their levels of government restrictions on religion and social hostilities involving religion. For 2013, see http://www.pewforum.org/2015/02/26/religious-hostilities/.

[19] Newbigin, *Trinitarian Doctrine for Today's Mission*, 84.

9

ON MISSION

Renewal of the doctrine of the Spirit is closely connected to renewal of our engagement in the mission of God.

A Church which has ceased to be a mission has lost the essential character of a Church.
—Lesslie Newbigin

Bring it on, Holy Spirit! Shake us up, send us forth, kick us out, and make us a more interesting church than we would be if you had left us alone?
—Stanley Hauerwas and William Willimon

We are presently on the far side of the church's long experience of Christendom. Many still long for the former privileged position the church occupied as a kind of chaplain to the culture. Some feel deep disorientation and distress. But George Hunsberger called this time a "wildly opportune moment" for churches to reclothe themselves in the garments of their calling.[1]

That reclothing involves breaking some long habits and questioning deep assumptions about the missional calling of Christians. It entails disentangling Christian discipleship from national citizenship. Also, it entails learning to conceive of the Christian community, not primarily as a vendor of Christian goods and services, but as a community birthed by the Spirit through the hearing and receiving of the gospel and living as gifted disciples representing the reign of God. In the power of the Spirit, the church is

God's contrast society, an alternative community modeling a new human-ity and called to be "a light to the nations."

Christendom, as we have seen, was not an alternative community or culture; it *was* the culture—and its strengths were offset by deep compro-mises. It produced a strong and steady stream of "alternative" voices and movements, to be sure: monasticism, orders like the Jesuits and Franciscans, and periodic renewal movements quickly judged "heretical" (like John Wycliffe and the Lollards in the fourteenth century and William Tyndale in the sixteenth) or dangerous and "enthusiastic" (like the Wesleyan move-ment in the eighteenth). And in America we have had a rambunctious Christian free-for-all, but moderated by a Christian mainstream viewing its role as maintaining a "Christian America."

Now that era is largely behind us. The West is a field of mission, and unmistakably so. We are on mission now—whether we know it or not.

The Church in the Presence of the Spirit

John Driver has highlighted a dozen biblical word pictures for the church that focus on its mission. He categorizes them into four groups:

1. Pilgrimage (sojourners, the way, the poor);
2. God's new order (kingdom of God, new creation, new humanity);
3. Peoplehood (family of God, people of God, shepherd and flock); and
4. Transformation (salt and light, spiritual house, witnessing community).

These rich images all point to a community that is set apart with a special vocation on behalf of all other peoples of the world, a community called to move throughout the world witnessing to the saving purposes of God.[2] The missional Spirit is its guiding presence and empowering force.

We now turn to consider some important features of the church in the presence of the Spirit of mission.

The Church as the Sphere of the Spirit's Power

Baptism as a Spirit event marks and empowers the transition into the new community of God called *church*. "For in one Spirit we were all baptized into one body—Jews or Greeks, slaves or free—and all were made to drink of one Spirit" (1 Cor. 12:13, ESV).

Baptism into the name of Father, Son, and Spirit identifies one with the life, death, and resurrection of Jesus (Rom. 6:1–4) and initiates one into a new community—the fellowship of the Spirit. In this fellowship one experiences ongoing conversion, repentance, gifting, and growth toward holiness. In early Christian communities, baptism in water was often followed by a rite of baptism in the Spirit, making explicit the reality of receiving the Spirit. Through faith in the Messiah and baptism in the Spirit (Rom. 6:2–5), God has broken the power of sin and death; the process of conforming believers' lives to the image of Christ has begun.

For Paul "the Holy Spirit is not an abstraction but the manifestation of God's presence in the community, making everything new. Those who respond to the gospel have entered the sphere of the Spirit's power, where they find themselves changed and empowered for obedience."[3] To enter the community of Christ is to enter the sphere of the Spirit's power. One of Paul's fundamental convictions is that the Spirit of God is active among groups of Christians (Rom. 15:19; Eph. 3:16; Gal. 3:5; 2 Tim. 1:7, 14, etc.).

Paul's approach to mission rests on this key point: "that the Holy Spirit of God is himself the missionary; that his presence and blessing are given to those who receive the gospel; that that presence and blessing are recognizable by those who have the Spirit; and that where the Spirit is, there is all the power and wisdom and grace that a person needs or can expect for the life in Christ."[4]

In the Spirit-filled community, as we saw in Chapter Six, there are mediating structures and "means" through which the Spirit works. These include the worshipping assembly, baptism and Lord's Supper, the public reading and teaching of Scripture, singing hymns and spiritual songs, fellowship in the tasks of ministry, and all kinds of prayer. In this Spirit-infused community—which is the New Temple of God—and through these means, "And we all, who with unveiled faces contemplate the Lord's glory, are being transformed into his image with ever-increasing glory, which comes from the Lord, who is the Spirit" (2 Cor. 3:18).

The Church as a Community of Broken Walls

God has made known his will in Christ "to be put into effect when the times reach their fulfillment—to bring unity to all things in heaven and on earth under Christ" (Eph. 1:10). A foretaste of that unity appears in the church, though it is fragmentary and provisional. It is a "unity of the Spirit through the bond of peace." It is a unity grounded in the one God—Spirit, Lord, and Father: there is "one body" just as there is "one Spirit . . . one Lord, one faith, one baptism, one God and Father of all" (Eph. 4:4–6). This is not a unity of uniformity or static sameness; indeed, as we are seeing around the world today, there is incredible diversity. In the New Testament, unity is a participation in and reflection of the communion of the Father, Son, and Spirit (John 17:21).

The call to unity in Paul's letters is a call for the pattern of Christ's self-giving love to be lived out in the Christian community (see Phil. 2:1–4). To further this call, the Spirit exposes and convicts us of our disunity—and not just between Christian denominations—but even more between rich and poor, black and white, cultural enclaves, and in-groups and out-groups of all kinds. In a deeply divided and tribal world where prejudices and animosity are deeply embedded, the church in the presence of the Spirit becomes a community of broken walls.

Humans have a strong propensity for wall building—walls of race, ethnicity, language, status, and age, all set deeply within cultural traditions. But the Spirit relentlessly presses us to breach the walls of tribe and clan and color and socioeconomics—indeed, to tear them down. So high are these walls and so deep their footings that the breaking down of them becomes an unmistakable sign of the Spirit's presence.

The Church as a Temple of the Spirit

The church is "marked with the seal of the promised Holy Spirit" (Eph. 1:13; 4:30) and described as "a holy temple in the Lord" where "you too are being built together to become a dwelling in which God lives by his Spirit" (2:21–22). For Paul the community of faith is "God's building" (1 Cor. 3:9), indeed, the building in which God dwells. "Do you not know that you [plural] are God's temple and that God's Spirit dwells in you [plural]?" (1 Cor. 3:16).

Paul's audacious point, as we have seen in Chapter Four, is that the Spirit-filled community is now where the glory of God resides, taking the place of the temple in Jerusalem. As these new temples spread out across the globe, the glory of God radiates to the nations. "Our task as a church is to be God's temple, so filled with his presence that we expand and fill the earth with that glorious presence until God finally accomplishes this goal completely at the end of time!"[5]

The Church as Proclaimer of the Words of Christ

The Spirit enables the church to bear witness to the gospel. We can say that the Spirit energizes Christian proclamation. While Peter and John were proclaiming Jesus' resurrection from the dead, they were seized and brought before the Jewish authorities who were "greatly disturbed" by the teaching. The healing of a lame beggar had also disturbed them, so they asked, "By what power or what name did you do this?" "Filled with the Holy Spirit," Peter answered, "It is by the name of Jesus Christ of Nazareth, whom you crucified but whom God raised from the dead. . . . Salvation is found in no one else" (Acts 4:7–12). Later when Peter addressed the large gathering in the house of Cornelius in Caesarea, proclaiming Jesus' anointing by the Spirit, his crucifixion, and resurrection, "the Holy Spirit came upon all who heard the message" (10:44).

Paul ascribes his own evangelistic effectiveness to the Spirit: "I will not venture to speak of anything except what Christ has accomplished through me in leading the Gentiles to obey God by what I have said and done—by the power of signs and wonders, through the power of the Spirit" (Rom. 15:18–19a). "Our gospel came to you not simply with words, but also with power, with the Holy Spirit, and deep conviction" (1 Thess. 1:5).

The Church as a Place of Transformation and Healing

Through the Spirit, God is creating communities that portray in advance, and begin to make visible, the forgiveness and healing of the world that began in the death and resurrection of Jesus. Through the Spirit, God is powerfully present in the church, transforming believers' lives and enabling them to live in a way that otherwise would be unattainable.

A key part of this transformation is the "renewing of your mind" (Rom. 12:2). This renewing process is fundamental since the basic human problem, according to Paul, is that we have become foolish and darkened in our thinking (Rom. 1:21). We need to be renewed in our thinking. "Think through who you really are in the crucified and risen Messiah," admonishes Paul (Rom. 6:11 KNT). Knowledge and discernment are integral to "abounding in love." There are thought-out and acquired habits of the mind that shape and guide our transformation in Christ.

Transformation through the Spirit includes the healing of the brokenness and disarray that we bring with us to Christ. We could picture the church as a hospital and rehab center—though it is much more than that. The fellowship of the Spirit contains people in various stages of healing and growth toward holiness. Some are just being wheeled into the emergency room, fresh from the wreck that has been their lives. Some are just out of radical surgery. Others are in need of strong medicine and intense care. Some are taking their first steps after lengthy incapacitation. Many are in need of the renewal of their minds, including training in the practices and truths of the faith. Some with the flush of health are going about their ordinary lives. And some are emerging as mature children of light and beginning to "shine like lights" in the darkness of the world.

The Church as Signpost, Foretaste, and Instrument of God's Reign

Lesslie Newbigin spoke of the church as "a signpost, a foretaste, and an instrument of the Kingdom of God."[6] Through the presence of the Holy Spirit, the church witnesses to the inbreaking of God's reign, tastes the banquet fare of the kingdom in advance, and becomes an instrument of God's kingdom by witnessing to and extending the ministry of Jesus.

As we have seen throughout this book, the Spirit brings "a provisional yet visible and concrete anticipation" of God's new age, God's future. The Spirit empowers the church to embody—in its mixed and very imperfect way—this new world coming. In the power of the Spirit, the church becomes a prototype, an early version, a signpost, of God's end-time community. It is, in fact, the place where heaven and earth are beginning to overlap. The church still groans in the midst of the old creation

(Rom. 8:20), but through the Spirit's presence experiences foretastes and signs of the new creation.

For Paul "new creation" serves as a shorthand for the basic eschatological tension that runs throughout the New Testament. The new creation already appears, but the "not yet" will not allow us to assert its unqualified presence. This tension provides the dynamism and energy for discipleship and mission in the present overlap of the ages. The receding of this tension, as we have seen, drives apart Spirit and mission and weakens the missional calling of the church. Patrick Mitchell puts it pointedly: "If the church loses Paul's razor-sharp awareness of the eschatological shape to the Christian life, the motive for mission and discipleship inevitably drains away."[7]

From Everywhere to Everywhere

I have developed a three-part thesis: (1) with the receding of (neo-) Christendom, a strong new focus on the mission of God has been emerging; (2) at the same time an unprecedented focus on the Holy Spirit has also emerged; and (3) the renewal of mission and of the Holy Spirit go hand in hand.

The Holy Spirit is calling and empowering Christians throughout the world to participate in God's mission. Some are called to become missionaries in the classical sense, leaving their home places and responding to the call of Christians in other places. After Christendom, no longer was this movement primarily from the dominant Christian West to the rest of the world, as it once was, but from "everywhere to everywhere." Now, as Newbigin predicted more than thirty years ago, mission movements are flowing from the Global South to the West—and all parts of the world. Today the movement of God's mission is truly from "everywhere to everywhere" or from "everywhere to everyone."

Some are called to become missionaries, yet all Christians are called to become missional—that is, to invest their lives in the mission of God. This means at least two basic things. First, it means that wherever we are, we bear witness to the forgiving, healing, freeing, and justice-bringing power of the gospel. Second, it means that all Christians are called into a worldwide vision of the people of God. It's a call to move beyond a Christian faith bounded by the loyalties and blinders of culture, tribe, and territory, and to participate in God's new people drawn from all tongues, tribes, and nations.

In the New Testament—and still today—the Spirit prompts a worldwide and cross-cultural vision of the kingdom of God. In first-century Antioch, Paul and Barnabas were called by the Spirit through the church leaders into a far-flung gospel mission: to make formation of a cross-cultural people their life work (Acts 13:1–3). Paul wrote of how Christ had broken down the walls that divided people—Jews and Gentiles, slaves and free people, insiders and outsiders—and was bringing a "new humanity" into being (Eph. 2:14–16). They were all baptized into one body through the one Spirit and were "all given the one Spirit to drink." With their many parts and vast differences, they were one body (1 Cor. 12:13, 19). Paul's great longing was to see everybody and all things gathered up through Christ into God's "new creation" (Eph. 1:10; Gal. 6:15).

Today the Spirit is leading us beyond the paternalism of the "wealthy" Western churches toward the "poor" churches of the Global South. The deep disparities between Western Christians as "donors"—of money, education, leadership, and other resources—and Christians of the Global South as "recipients" of all those gifts is beginning to give way to a new sense of interdependence and mutuality. In all places the church is both gifted and needy. The churches of the Global South have deep needs and possess great gifts, while the churches of the West also have deep needs and possess great gifts. And it may be that the needs of the Western churches are greater than those in the South. In the (post)modern West, Christians are beset by rationalism, deep skepticism toward the Spirit of God, the snares of affluence and consumerism, their own version of cultural syncretism (the deep blending of the faith with secular ideologies), and the heritage of cultural dominance that is the legacy of Christendom. So the churches of each region need the strengths, gifts, and correctives of the other.[8]

In his many travels to study churches in South America and Africa, Donald Miller, a Christian sociologist, commented that after every trip "I have come back humbled by my lack of faith, my own failure of imagination, and my resistance to commit myself to the high standard of being a servant of Christ." He added that "[w]e in North America live in a bubble of affluence and convenience, and this [deeply] affects our theology."[9] In these extensive travels, Miller received a powerful gift from the churches of the Global South.

Another gift is a more missional theology. The churches of the Christendom centuries were not fundamentally churches on mission. And their theologies, understandably, were not missional theologies. Missions may have been one department in the seminary curriculum, one chapter in a book of theology, or one ministry of a congregation—but mission did not animate, infuse, and shape the whole enterprise. In the Global South the situation has changed. With the dynamic renewal of the missional Spirit, new missional theologies have emerged as well. "Third World theologies are missionary theologies, whereas First World theologies are not," said David Bosch more than twenty years ago; for this reason, "Third World theologies may become a force of renewal in the West."[10] That has been happening. This renewal is one of the Global South's gifts to the church in the West.

With the recent and growing sense of North America as mission field, a strong movement toward a dynamic missional theology has emerged. Lesslie Newbigin helped pioneer this focus, and it has been furthered by the Gospel and Our Culture Network and a growing body of literature since the 1990s.[11] A missional theology has been emerging alongside the traditional theology that may have been limited to a chapter on missions.

A dynamic focus on the Spirit goes hand in hand with a dynamic mission. So a missional theology will necessarily have a strong focus on the missional Spirit of God. And vice versa: a strong focus on the Spirit of God leads necessarily to the church engaged dynamically in the mission of God.

Gifted Leaders for Mission

In Ephesians, the apostle describes the path of maturity in Christ. We find the common creed that binds the church together, despite the obvious fact that we are all different: "one body and one Spirit. . . one Lord, one faith, one baptism; one God and Father of all, who is over all and through all and in all" (Eph. 4:4–6).

Christ also gives diverse gifts through the Spirit so the church can grow into maturity and carry out its mission. "The gifts he gave" Paul writes, "were that some would be apostles, some prophets, some evangelists, some pastors and teachers," (Eph. 4:11, NRSV). When these gifted leaders embody and practice their gifts, the whole church is awakened and becomes mature "attaining to the whole measure of the fullness of Christ" (4:13). And conversely, the writer seems to be saying that without such diverse equipping, leaders in communities will not be able to mature and well represent the full mission of Christ.

The first two gifts, apostle and prophet, have tended to be dismissed as no longer valid. Apostles were special eyewitnesses and miracle-working followers of Jesus, and prophets were those who spoke an inspired and unerring word from God. A common view is that all five ministry gifts of Ephesians 4:11 were given by the ascended Christ to the church near its beginning but that not all of them continue today. Some hold that only the gifts of evangelist, pastor, and teacher continue today; others that only the gifts of pastor and teacher remain. These leadership and equipping functions are surely needed in every generation, and it is not a natural reading of the passage to assume that there is a distinction between gifts that should continue and gifts that should not.[12]

Apostle

The word means "messenger" or "sent one." I suggest that in Ephesians this refers not so much to a title but to a characteristic and a task, a role, or function, not an "office." To speak of the church as apostolic is to affirm its missionary calling, that it is a people sent out on God's mission. So apostolic as a characteristic of the church has a double sense: it points to the church's *foundation* on the first eyewitness apostles, and it points to the church's *commission* to carry out the apostolic task. So the apostolic task, in this second sense, is carried out by people gifted and called to mission in a focused way.[13] They are effective church planters and pioneers of mission. In this broad sense, the apostolic gifting is the Spirit-given impulse to take the gospel into new places, to cross settled boundaries. People gifted in this way are pioneers and visionaries who are always seeking forward movement in God's mission. They like to live on the rugged frontiers of mission.

Prophet

This word also has tended to be dropped out of the Christian vocabulary. The concept of prophet and prophetic gifts in the church has been a contested one. Let me suggest a way to reclaim this—and how it can help us as we learn to minister from the margins. This gifting can be seen in people who are especially sensitive to the prompting of the Spirit. They can discern God's work in peoples' lives that most may not see. They call us back to foundational things when we seem to be getting off track. They are often questioners and agitators readily challenging the status quo, so they often come across as troublemakers and dreamers. They usually demonstrate a strong calling to serve the poor and disenfranchised.

Evangelists

These are the ones who are consistently passionate about connecting with people who don't know Jesus. They talk easily about Jesus with people, and there is almost nothing they enjoy more. And they refuse to let the church remain inwardly focused. When an evangelist becomes part of a leadership team, he or she is always asking, "What are we doing to connect with people outside our church and outside of Christ?"

Shepherd/Pastor

Shepherds or pastors have a deep heart for human brokenness and long to bring healing and wholeness to people. Their impulse is to care for people. They feel the weight of struggling marriages. They are attuned to the sick and hurting. They tend to know when people aren't doing well. And they want to see the church as a whole respond well to hurting people.

Teacher

The teacher's passion is to help a congregation become immersed in Scripture and learn how to live out of its story. Teachers seek to feed the hunger for God's Word. They create and gather resources for congregational

Bible study. They tend to be interested in things like tools for Bible study, commentaries, current theological trends, and doctrinal controversies. Sometimes they tend to think that most of a congregation's problems could be solved by more and better Bible study. Some seek to teach people how to pray, how to worship, how to live in community, how to construct a "rule of life," and how to live missionally.

Churches in our time have grown comfortable with shepherds/pastors and with teachers. Those are the leaders who tend to be called into congregational leadership. But "apostle" types, "prophet" types, even "evangelist" types—many churches have not quite known what to do with such people when they show up. So these people have tended to exercise their gifts outside the congregation. The "apostle" types are out pioneering parachurch organizations, the "prophet" types are leading social justice ministries, and the "evangelist" types are spearheading new thrusts to reach campuses and cities.

What if a congregation decided to make room for all five types of gifted leaders? What if a leadership team intentionally sought a greater diversity of gifting?

If we recognize that Christian churches in North America and in the West are in a new missional situation, and if we want to think and function more like congregations on mission, then we will want to seek a more diverse mix of gifted leaders—not only pastors and teachers but also those with gifts that keep us turning outward and calling us to the S/spirit of risk and adventure.

Living on Mission

What might it mean to live on God's mission in the power of the Spirit in this time and this place? Here are some concluding suggestions.

Learn to Live as Diaspora Communities

Early Christians spoke of themselves as "alien citizens." This image has deep roots in the New Testament. God's great people of faith acknowledged that they were "strangers and exiles on the earth" (Heb. 11:13, ESV). Christians are "aliens and exiles," Peter says; nonetheless they must "be subject for the Lord's sake to every human institution" (1 Pet. 2:11–14, ESV). Though they are a colony of heaven, they live and patiently serve in this world (Phil. 3:20).

During the first three centuries, the Christian church maintained a strong sense of being "resident aliens"—diaspora communities. But the fourth century, as we have seen, began an era where this sense of being strangers and exiles diminished. That sense is being renewed in this season. Christian faith is taking on more the character of diaspora communities around the world.

Instead of just letting ourselves be forced to the margins and wondering what happened, we can seek to learn what it means to live in the marginal or liminal spaces of our time. That's where discipleship thrives. That's where the Spirit's gifts flourish. That's where the giftedness of each and every church member can emerge. That's where the adventure of mission ramps up.

A good model of diaspora is the one Jeremiah set forth to the Israelites in Babylon. Like the Jewish exiles after the fall of Jerusalem, many Christians in the West are struggling with dislocation and grieving their losses. The passing of (neo-)Christendom has left many feeling vulnerable and disoriented. The Lord said through the prophet Jeremiah, "seek the welfare of the city where I have sent you into exile" (Jer. 29:7, ESV). So like Israel we build our houses and plant our gardens, and marry and raise children as though we are in our homeland—but we are not in our homeland. Richard Neuhaus refers to this as "our awkward duality of citizenship." On the one hand, it is tempting to sink one's roots down in foreign soil and simply let it be home; on the other hand, one can be constricted by fear or paralyzed by the grief of exile.

Worship is the key place we get formed in this "awkward" way. The elements of worship can direct us mostly inward with attention on ourselves and the comforting benefits of grace, or the same elements can turn us outward to the horizon of the city and the world and the brokenness around us. For one thing, I suggest we sing more exile songs. "The best Christian songs are songs . . . that acknowledge the exilic nature of the Church in the world. Here we have no lasting home, so our hymns can have the timbre of exile—the grief, the anger, the wrestling with God, the joy that is fierce and defiant rather than safe and smiley."[14] Such practices week by week can steadily form a mission-oriented community.

Live into the Big Story of God's Mission

At the center of this formation is learning to live out of the story that defines who Christians are. That big story is the long and richly textured story of Israel and its climax in the Messiah's ministry, death, resurrection, and ascension, and in Pentecost.

We are all, whether we know it or not, defined by big stories. The story of America. The story of Western capitalism and progress. The story of rugged individualism. These big stories are supplemented by smaller, more local stories, and together these stories form us at deep, mostly unconscious levels. In Charles Taylor's phrase, they create one's "social imaginary," one's reflexive way of being in the world.

Christians have an alternative story, and it stands in sharp contrast to the big stories that shape the modern West—the story of empire, of progress, of the sovereign individual. It's the big story that spans the whole canon of Scripture, climaxing with Jesus and Pentecost and the renewal of Israel's mission to the nations. To live into this big story, to see oneself as a participant in this story, is to put on a missional identity.

So the carefully planned reading of Scripture in worship, as we saw in Chapter Six, is constantly situating us in this story—from Torah to Prophets to Writings to Gospels to Epistles to Apocalypse. And preaching should be narrative preaching—that is, steadily opening up that story, connecting us to that story, and showing how Christ stands at the center of the story.

This is what the Holy Spirit did among the earliest Christians as they encountered and proclaimed the good news about Jesus. In the New Testament the Holy Spirit "anchors an understanding of Jesus to the Scriptures of Israel"; thus a key vocation of the Spirit in the church is "to illuminate the person of Jesus by setting his words and actions in the context of Israel's poetry, stories, and prophecies."[15]

In this way the Spirit helps us to live into God's grand story and out of it into mission.

Open Oneself to the Spirit

The Spirit is the driving energy of new creation. For those who confess Christ and "receive" the Spirit, the Spirit endows with power and equips for ministry. For some believers there may be a sudden, powerful endowment. But this endowment doesn't necessarily happen all at once. We can grow in our openness and attentiveness to the Spirit.

Openness is a posture that one can assume. And of course opposition can be one's stance. Or indifference. Openness, we can say, is a "human variable. Response runs the gamut from unbelief to unrestricted surrender (Mark 6:5; Acts 4:29–30)."[16] The Spirit can be received in fuller ways by believers (Eph. 5:18), but can also be grieved (Eph. 4:30), resisted (Acts 7:51), quenched (1 Thess. 5:19), even insulted (Heb. 10:29).

Though the Holy Spirit is already within us and among us, the Spirit can fill us anew. "Keep on being filled with the Spirit," Paul exhorted. This imperative certainly applies to individuals, but in the context of Ephesians it applies especially to the community of faith—so that its worship (psalms, hymns, and Spirit songs) and life together (submitting to one another) give full evidence of the Spirit's presence.

The Spirit's filling can awaken us to greater and fuller dimensions of God's love, to greater longing for the reign of God and thus the peace of God to fill the earth. The gift of the Spirit in baptism may need to be more fully received, more richly experienced. We may need to break through barriers in our lives, places where we are stuck in immaturity and constricting habits. We may need to have our hearts further enlightened, to taste the heavenly gift and the goodness of God's Word more fully, and to experience more of the powers of the age to come (Heb. 6:4–5). We may need the renewing of our minds in order to be more established in our faith—and perhaps to get past worldview barriers that, in the West, keep us so suspicious and unmindful of the Spirit.

We need more of the Spirit's power in order to be disciples, to be God's "royal priesthood" in the mending of a broken and still groaning creation.

But openness to the Spirit is risky, for the Spirit is no shy or tame Spirit. Roger Olson asks, "Does this make you nervous? It should. The Holy Spirit is not predictable or safe. The Holy Spirit shatters the status quo, breaking us out of complacency and lifting us up to new heights of spiritual fullness and blessing—if we are open to that."[17]

Pray in the Spirit

The Spirit plays a pivotal role in prayer—and prayer a pivotal role in mission. Paul exhorts: "And pray in the Spirit on all occasions with all kinds of prayers and requests. With this in mind, be alert and always keep on praying for all the saints" (Eph. 6:18; cf. Jude 20–21, "[by] praying in the Holy Spirit, keep yourselves in God's love"). The Ephesians passage speaks of wielding the sword of the Spirit (6:17) then immediately of "praying in the Spirit" (6:18). Gordon Fee connects the two imperatives around the weaponry metaphor. Thus prayer in the Spirit becomes "the final expression of Christian weaponry in the conflict with the 'powers.'"[18] It is a way of engaging in spiritual battle. It is a kind of prayer in which the Spirit takes on a deep empowering role. Paul wants them to "pray in the Spirit" for himself, that he will be bold in making known the mystery of the gospel (6:19).

Praying in the Spirit, no doubt, takes numerous forms. One was suggested by John Miller, who contrasted "frontline prayer" with "maintenance prayer." Maintenance prayer focuses on maintaining the present life of the church, the status quo; frontline prayer calls boldly for God to act in mighty and life-changing ways, for the Spirit to empower and guide a congregation in carrying out God's mission to heal and renew and to engage the powers that stand against God's kingdom. Frontline prayer is outward focused and expects God to act.[19]

Drawing on this distinction between maintenance and frontline prayer, Tim Keller draws out what he sees as three particular aspects of frontline prayer. It is prayer (1) for grace to confess sins and to humble ourselves; (2) for compassion and zeal for the flourishing of the church and the reaching of the lost; and (3) for yearning to know God, to see God's face, and to glimpse God's glory.[20]

Frontline prayer—a form of praying in the Spirit—is the prayer of the church on mission.

Leave the House

Today many assume that it is possible to serve God without ever leaving the house or the church building. We can listen to the best preachers on their podcasts and to our favorite worship music on our iPhones. We can worship in online church services or at least the parts that suit our tastes. We can engage global issues on the Internet through "click activism." We can avoid or minimize the messiness of community with real people and their irritating issues by carefully limiting our involvement in face-to-face events. This is the trendy way of excarnation.

The way of Jesus is the way of incarnation, the way of flesh and blood. The Spirit befriends our bodies. We are formed as Jesus' disciples in and as our bodies. So, as Michael Frost says, "We need to get out of the house. . . . We need to develop joint practices or habits with like-minded followers of Jesus that bind us more deeply to God, to each other, and which propel us outward into the lives of others, especially the poor, the lost and the lonely."[21]

In a TED talk a few years ago, Ben Saunders, a modern-day polar explorer, asked the question, "Why bother leaving the house?" In a wired age when most anything you want to know or to buy is available at your fingertips, it's a good question. One of his feats was walking on the ice from one side of the Arctic Circle to the other. He was asked why people should bother to attempt such feats.

"If I've learned anything from nearly twelve years of dragging heavy things around cold places," he replied, "it's that true, real inspiration and growth only comes from adversity and challenge, from stepping away from what's comfortable and familiar and stepping out into the unknown."[22]

The Spirit calls and gifts us disciples for the adventure of God's kingdom coming. And the focus of the Spirit's work, as we have seen, is on and through persons-in-community, flesh and blood people on whom the Spirit has come to rest.

So join with some of those Spirit people. Mix it up with them. Make friends. Venture into the highways and byways with them. Get your hands dirty and your body tired. Weep over brokenness with them. Receive the hurting without judgment. Lose yourself. Carry someone. Bless the fearful and the cynical.

The Spirit has been poured out. So take some risks. And then some more. Pray in the Spirit, on the frontlines. Participate in new creation. Rest, and worship to high heaven. Testify to joy, and to Jesus.

The Spirit will form you. The Spirit will sustain you.

NOTES

[1] George Hunsberger, "Missional Vocation," in *Missional Church: A Vision for the Sending of the Church in North America*, ed. Darrell Guder (Grand Rapids: Eerdmans, 1998), 78.

[2] John Driver, *Images of the Church in Mission* (Scottdale, PA: Herald, 1997).

[3] Richard Hays, *The Moral Vision of the New Testament: A Contemporary Introduction to New Testament Ethics* (New York: HarperCollins, 1996), 45.

[4] Lesslie Newbigin, *Trinitarian Doctrine for Today's Mission* (1988; Wipf & Stock, 2006), 71.

[5] G. K. Beale, "Eden, the Temple, and the Church's Mission in the New Creation," *Journal of Evangelical Theological Studies* 48 (March 2005): 31.

[6] Lesslie Newbigin, "The Church: A Bunch of Escaped Convicts," *Reform* (June 1990): 6.

[7] Patrick Mitchell, "The New Perspective on the Christian Life: *Solus Spiritus*," in *The Apostle Paul and the Christian Life*, ed. Scot McKnight and Joseph Modica (Grand Rapids: Baker Academic, 2016), 97.

[8] Lesslie Newbigin, *Foolishness to the Greeks* (Grand Rapids: Eerdmans, 1986), chapter 9, and "Can the West Be Converted?" *Princeton Seminary Bulletin* 6 (1985): 25–36; and Alan Kreider and Eleanor Kreider, *Worship and Mission after Christendom* (Scottdate, PA: Herald, 2011), 196–98.

[9] Donald E. Miller, "Emergent Patterns of Congregational Life and Leadership in the Developing World: Personal Reflections from a Research Odyssey," *Pulpit and Pew Research Reports*, No. 3 (Winter 2003), 9.

[10] David Bosch, *Believing in the Future: Toward a Missiology of Western Culture* (Valley Forge, PA: Trinity International, 1995), 36.

[11] Two key works were *Between Gospel and Culture: The Emerging Mission in North America*, ed. George R. Hunsberger and Craig Van Gelder (Grand Rapids: Eerdmans, 1996), and Darryl Guder, ed., *Missional Church: A Vision for the Sending of the Church in North America* (Grand Rapids: Eerdmans 1998).

[12] On the fivefold gifting, see Alan Hirsch and Michael Frost, *The Shaping of Things to Come: Innovation and Mission for the 21st-Century Church*, revised and updated (Grand Rapids: Baker, 2013), 205–45; and J. R. Briggs and Bob Hyatt, *Eldership and the Mission of God: Equipping Teams for Faithful Church Leadership* (Downers Grove, IL: InterVarsity, 2015), 111–28.

[13] Note that the New Testament uses the word "apostle" to refer to leaders beyond the original twelve (see Rom. 16:7; 1 Thess. 1:1, 2:6; Acts 14:14; 2 Cor. 8:23; Phil. 2:25).

[14] Alexi Sargeant, "Songs of Exile," *First Things* (June 2016), accessed November 1, 2017, https://www.firstthings.com/blogs/firstthoughts/2016/06/songs-of-exile.

[15] John Levison, *Fresh Air: The Holy Spirit for an Inspired Life* (Brewster, MA: Paraclete, 2012), 210.

[16] Clark Pinnock, *Flame of Love: A Theology of the Holy Spirit* (Downers Grove, IL: InterVarsity, 1996), 137.

[17] Roger Olson, "The Holy Spirit: Shy Member of the Trinity?" sermon, May 2016.

[18] Gordon Fee, *God's Empowering Presence: The Holy Spirit in the Letters of Paul* (Peabody, MA: Hendrickson, 1994), 730.

[19] C. John Miller, *Outgrowing the Ingrown Church* (Grand Rapids: Zondervan, 1986), 100.

[20] Tim Keller, *Center Church: Doing Balanced, Gospel-Centered Ministry in Your City* (Grand Rapids: Zondervan, 2012), 73.

[21] Michael Frost, *Incarnate: The Body of Christ in an Age of Disengagement* (Downers Grove, IL: InterVarsity, 2014), 146.

[22] "Why Bother Leaving the House?" TED talk, quoted in Frost, *Incarnate*, 147.

AFTERWORD

The church in which I grew up lacked a grammar for talking about the Spirit, but still there were signs of the forming presence of the Spirit, especially in the "spiritual songs" that we sang with vigor and, sometimes, with joy.

My father was an elder in this church for many years. When I was born, he was forty-three. In most ways, our lives did not intersect. He did not play ball with me. He never fished with me. He did not attend any of my sporting events—from little league to high school track to varsity basketball.

The dinner table provided the forum for my main encounters with my dad. It was the place I was grilled and drilled on three topics of primary importance to him: healthy food, the true church, and correct grammar. In that order.

I got the grammar down really well. The other stuff wasn't so easy.

My father was obsessed with health and healthy food. The centerpiece of his morning kitchen ritual was mixing up a thick, viscous concoction that my parents called "tiger's milk." To the ordinary person who had the misfortune of tasting it, the drink was vile—literally undrinkable due to the gag reflex.

I drank tiger's milk from the time I was five or six until I left my parents' house to go to college at age sixteen.

Tiger's milk represented a set of deep convictions—never fully articulated—about how life was to be lived in this world. There was a right way to eat and a wrong way to eat, and following the right way was part of one's duty to God.

Mealtime around my dad's table was mostly a time for ingesting a carefully calibrated assortment of whole foods and supplements for the purpose of maintaining physical health—and holiness. In the house of my childhood there were no "feasts," no festive gatherings of friends where food and drink become sacraments of joy and friendship.

A little boy didn't quite know what to make of this. I strove with all my might to learn the healthy doctrine and to live by the code. But it wasn't long until I was inducted into the clandestine joys of forbidden food: ice cream sandwiches, Oreo cookies, French fries, Cokes. My school friends—with their families' unenlightened dietary habits—were the primary culprits.

I was always the model boy and the model teenager—the one that the mothers at church always bragged about as the epitome of manners and maturity. I was kind, respectful of my parents and others, an excellent student, and conscientious in all my ways—and doubly so when it came to my desire to follow God.

But by age fifteen, I began to sense cracks and tremors in the true church edifice that was tied so integrally to our family's moral and dietary rules. My questions launched me not only on an intellectual quest through my college years but on a theological career. I needed to know where the type of Christianity that had been so deeply instilled in me came from. I had been told since childhood that it came simply and solely from the Bible.

Through years of seminary and doctoral work in Bible and historical theology, I learned otherwise. The discoveries were exciting and invigorating, but sometimes troubling, even wrenching.

Some years into my academic career, a private personal crisis precipitated in me what I would call a spiritual collapse. It would fit in the category of what John of the Cross famously called a "dark night of the soul." There are various species of that genus; mine had deep roots in the story you've glimpsed here.

It thrust me into a desert season.

Lots of things get lost and stripped away in the desert. Things that once seemed impressive and important wither and blow away. In the desert one may well cross over into the realm of the Other. The realm of the broken and pitiable ones, the unpresentable or scandalous ones. The ones outside the camp. In the desert one begins to know oneself as Other. And as that happens, the world begins to look different.

When I began to emerge from the desert I found myself a different person.

There—what can I call it?—I began to learn how to dance.

This is certainly an odd image for a boy with my upbringing. All through the elementary years I sat out every single square dance at my school, and all through high school and college I never attended a single dance. I had been taught since childhood that all dancing was off limits for true Christians. I even got the impression that fornication was off limits mainly because it could lead to dancing. As an adult, the very muscles in my legs seemed to be wired with a deep inhibition against it.

My first time ever to set foot on a dance floor was when I escorted my lovely and graceful high school daughter to the annual father-daughter banquet. There, to my embarrassment, I found myself on the dance floor trying to move my body to the sounds of that classic song "Who Let the Dogs Out?"

Slowly I've been learning to dance.

This is a metaphor that emerged early in the Christian tradition to depict the Trinity. The image of a divine dance was used to portray the dynamic intermingling, the mutual submission, the perfect harmony, and perfect love in the life of Father, Spirit, and Son.

Through the Spirit of God we are invited to share in this life. A life so wonderful and rich that joy permeates it. And so perfect that it reaches down into our very deepest longings. Call it life in the Spirit.

It is an invitation to dance.

I suspect that every little child, at some point, experiences that invitation in some way, and dances a round with God. But the memory of that dance easily and often fades, and gets put away with childish things if there is no language provided to name it, no words to affirm and illumine it.[1]

As my father had well taught me long ago, I was not allowed to dance. Even as I would hear the music and long to step into the rhythms, my feet would tangle and my heart would shrink.

But for these past couple of decades, I have been learning to dance. Several years ago, I gave my wife dancing lessons as a birthday gift. Country dancing—the two-step. It looked easy enough. Who could mess up two steps? As I joined her as a partner, I quickly learned there was a lot more to it than two steps. There was knowing which way to turn, how to swing her around in various ways, when to go backward, and when to go forward. We eventually did some serious boot scooting. But it was frustrating. And exhilarating.

Through it all I just couldn't seem to get the inhibitions worked out of my muscles.

But I have been learning to dance. It's quiet and slow, often awkward, rarely elegant. But the deep and joyful rhythms of grace sound loud and clear, and I'm stepping out with them. I keep training my legs (kneeling is good) and limbering my arms (raising them is good) and lifting my heart (confessing my sin and my faith is good) and joining with beloved brothers and sisters (fellowship is good).

The desert season remains an important and ever-present marker. I consider it a dark and necessary grace. As we know from Scripture, deserts are places of testing, refining, and preparation. And so it was for me.

Once in a while I think back to mealtime around my father's table all those years ago. But it's not my table anymore. No more tiger's milk for me; rather, it's the sacraments of food and friendship, of bread and brotherhood, of laughter and love. And around the table of the Lord, it's the encounter with the invisible but real presence of Jesus, who is real food and real drink—a taste of the Spirit of resurrection life.

I believe with David Hart that life in the Spirit, for the most part, is one of steadiness, calm, sobriety, lucidity, and joy. That we "pray . . . with constancy of will and a patient openness to grace, suffering states of both dereliction and ecstasy with the equanimity of faith."[2]

This, for me, is life in the Spirit.

NOTES

[1]An image suggested by Walter Wangerin, *The Orphean Passages* (Grand Rapids: Zondervan, 1986), 11–12.

[2]David Bentley Hart, *The Experience of God: Being, Consciousness, Bliss* (New Haven, CT: Yale University, 2013), 327–28.

FOR FURTHER READING

Allen, C. Leonard. *The Cruciform Church: Becoming a Cross-Shaped People in a Secular World*. Anniversary edition. Abilene, TX: Abilene Christian University, 2016.

Beale, G. K. *The Temple and the Church's Mission: A Biblical Theology of the Dwelling Place of God*. Downers Grove, IL: InterVarsity, 2004.

Burke, Trevor J. *Adopted into God's Family: Exploring a Pauline Metaphor*. Downers Grove, IL: InterVarsity, 2007.

Fee, Gordon. *Paul, the Spirit, and the People of God*. Peabody, MA: Hendrickson, 1994.

Frost, Michael. *Incarnate: The Body of Christ in an Age of Disengagement*. Downers Grove, IL: InterVarsity, 2014.

Goheen, Michael. *A Light to the Nations: The Missional Church and the Biblical Story*. Grand Rapids: Baker Academic, 2011.

Greenman, Jeffrey P., and George Kalantzis, eds. *Life in the Spirit: Spiritual Formation in Theological Perspective*. Downers Grove, IL: IVP Academic, 2010.

Hauerwas, Stanley, and William Willimon. *The Holy Spirit*. Nashville: Abingdon, 2015.

Karkkainen, Veli-Matti. *The Holy Spirit: A Guide to Christian Theology*. Louisville, KY: Westminster John Knox, 2012.

Levison, John R. *Fresh Air: The Holy Spirit for an Inspired Life*. Brewster, MA: Paraclete, 2012.

Noll, Mark. *The New Shape of World Christianity*. Downers Grove, IL: InterVarsity Academic, 2009.

Packer, James. *Keep in Step with the Spirit*. Downers Grove, IL: InterVarsity, 1984.

Parry, Robin A. *Worshipping Trinity: Coming Back to the Heart of Worship*. 2nd edition. Eugene, OR: Cascade, 2012.

Smith, James K. A. *Desiring the Kingdom: Worship, Worldview, and Cultural Formation*. Grand Rapids: Baker Academic, 2009.

Sundquist, Scott. *Understanding Christian Mission: Participation in Suffering and Glory*. Grand Rapids: Baker Academic, 2013.

Thistleton, Anthony. *A Shorter Guide to the Holy Spirit*. Grand Rapids: Eerdmans, 2016.

Warrington, Keith. *Discovering the Holy Spirit in the New Testament*. Peabody, MA: Hendrickson, 2005.

Wright, Christopher J. H. *The Mission of God: Unlocking the Bible's Grand Narrative*. Downers Grove, IL: InterVarsity, 2006.

Resources

THE APOSTLES' CREED

This creed is rooted in the baptismal liturgies of the second and third centuries, though this specific form emerged within the Western church in various editions from the fourth to the eighth centuries.

I BELIEVE in God, the Father almighty, creator of heaven and earth.

I believe in Jesus Christ, his only Son, our Lord.
He was conceived by the power of the Holy Spirit
and born of the Virgin Mary.

He suffered under Pontius Pilate,
was crucified, died, and was buried.

He descended to the dead.
On the third day he rose again.
He ascended into heaven,
and is seated at the right hand of the Father.

He will come again to judge the living and the dead.

I believe in the Holy Spirit,
the holy catholic Church,
the communion of saints,
the forgiveness of sins,
the resurrection of the body,
and the life everlasting.

Amen.

THE NICENE CREED

This creed was produced by the Council of Nicaea in AD 325 and amended by the Council of Constantinople in AD 381.

We believe in one God,
    the Father, the Almighty,
    maker of heaven and earth,
    of all that is, seen and unseen.

And in one Lord Jesus Christ,
    the only Son of God,
    begotten from the Father before all ages,
    God from God,
    Light from Light,
    true God from true God,
    begotten, not made;
    of the same essence as the Father.
    Through him all things were made.

For us and for our salvation
    he came down from heaven:
    by the power of the Holy Spirit
    he became incarnate from the Virgin Mary,
    and was made man.

*[He was baptized by John the Baptist, and filled with the Spirit:
    to preach the kingdom of God to the poor,
    to heal the sick,
    to receive those who have been cast out,

to revive Israel for the salvation of the nations, and
to have mercy upon all people.]
Addition by Jürgen Moltmann (1989)

For our sake he was crucified under Pontius Pilate;
    he suffered death and was buried.
    On the third day he rose again
    in accordance with the Scriptures;
    he ascended into heaven
    and is seated at the right hand of the Father.

He will come again in glory to judge
    the living and the dead,
    and his kingdom will have no end.

We believe in the Holy Spirit,
    the Lord, the giver of life,
    who proceeds from the Father.
    With the Father and the Son
    he is worshiped and glorified.
    He has spoken through the Prophets.

We believe in one holy catholic and apostolic Church.
We acknowledge one baptism for the forgiveness of sins.
We look for the resurrection of the dead,
    and the life of the world to come.

Amen.

ON THE HOLY SPIRIT

Patriarch Ignatius IV

When Patriarch Ignatius IV (1920–2012) addressed the World Council
of Churches in 1968, he shared these words about the Holy Spirit.

Without the Holy Spirit, God is far away,
Christ stays in the past,
the Gospel is a dead letter,
the Church is simply an organization,
authority a matter of domination,
mission a matter of propaganda,
liturgy is only nostalgia,
and Christian living a slave morality.

But with the Holy Spirit,
God is with us,
the universe is resurrected and groans
with the birth pangs of the kingdom,
the risen Christ is here,
the Gospel is a living force,
the Church is a communion
in the life of the Trinity—
the body of the living Christ—
authority is a service that liberates people,
mission is Pentecost,
the liturgy is memory and anticipation,
and human action is God's work in the world.

PENTECOST PRAYER FOR A CONFINED SPIRIT

Mandy Smith

Father,

Thank you that when the body of Jesus left this earth,
    He breathed Your Spirit into His Body.
Thank you for Your promise to be with us always,
That we have fellowship with You in a place no earthly power
    can touch.

Over centuries and continents that Spirit has guided
    and comforted and preached.
That Spirit has been faithful. And powerful. And unstoppable.

But the container has overcome the thing contained.
The clay jar has forgotten its own fragility,
    trivialized the treasure it holds.

We have felt the immensity of the call,
    seen the threats that surround.
And we have turned to our own strength.
We have oppressed and excluded.
We have puffed ourselves up with knowledge,
    used your Word as a weapon.
We have become professionals, overseeing systems; politicians,
    aligned with human powers.

We have perfected ourselves, filled ourselves up,
Crowded out the Spirit's dwelling.

Who has any need for Your Spirit when we are so strong,
    so capable?

The Spirit grieves in that confinement,
Waiting, pensive, pressing:
A force of love and longing, ever seeking a way,
Ever watching, writhing to be freed to the aching world.

May Your Spirit be revealed in all the color and
    personality of each person in Your Body.
May Your Spirit be seen through the unique flavor of
    each local community.
Let Your Spirit be spoken through every poet's pen.
Let Your Spirit flow through the hands of every artist.
Let Your Spirit loosen the tongue of every singer, every preacher.
Let every child dance to that rhythm, every old man tap his toes.

Whatever Your Spirit wants to heal, let it be healed.
Whatever Your Spirit wants to free, let it be freed.

Help us empty ourselves of ourselves,
So that whatever small, cramped piece of Spirit is still within us
May swell to the fullness of Your beauty and strength.

May Your Spirit be unleashed in and through us,
Because of us and in spite of us.
So Your Body may live and breathe again.

Amen